Prehistoric Preseli

a field guide

N.P. Figgis

*

*Designed and produced
by Helen Walker*

Published 2001
by ATELIER PRODUCTIONS
2, Bontfaen, Forge,
Machynlleth, Powys SY20 8RN

ISBN 1 899793 06 2

Reprinted 2003

British Library Cataloguing-in-Publication Data
A catalogue record for this book is
available from the British Library

CONTENTS

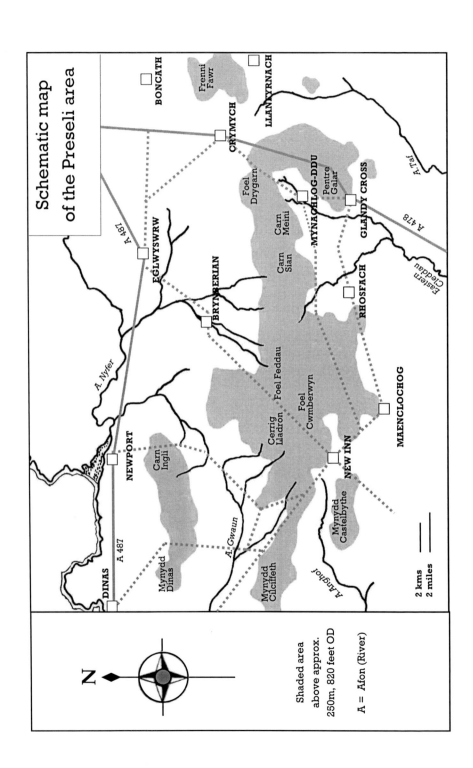

Schematic map
of the Preseli area

N

Shaded area
above approx.
250m, 820 feet OD

A = Afon (River)

2 kms
2 miles

DINAS
A 487
NEWPORT
Carn
Ingli
Mynydd
Dinas
A. Nyfer
A. Gwaun
Mynydd
Cilciffeth
A. Anghof
Mynydd
Castelbythe
NEW INN
Foel
Cwmberwyn
Cerrig
Lladron
Foel Feddau
MAENCLOCHOG
RHOSFACH
BRYNBERIAN
EGLWYSWRW
A 487
Carn
Sian
Carn
Meini
Foel
Drygarn
CRYMYCH
BONCATH
Frenni
Fawr
LLANYRNACH
MYNACHLOG-DDU
Pentre
Galar
GLANDY CROSS
A 478
Eastern
Cleddau
A. Taf

INTRODUCTION

Preseli is one of Britain's special places, to those who have lived here in the remote past, to those who live here now, and to the many who come to visit. It has provided hunting-ground and farm, fortress and burial place for thousands of years. This little book is offered as a simple guide to the monuments and remains with which the people of prehistory enhanced it.

We have divided the book into two parts: a brief explanation of Preseli's prehistoric heritage in its contemporary context, and a Gazetteer of the most informative sites. Numbers in bold type in the main body of the text refer to a Gazetteer entry. Only a proportion of the recorded prehistoric sites have been included; there are many more, some of them so slight as to be virtually invisible, and many which are of uncertain date and/or authenticity. (The complete record is held by the Dyfed Archaeological Trust, which welcomes serious enquiries). New sites are found, excavated and published every year; and, just as significantly, known material is constantly being reviewed and re-interpreted in the light of fresh discoveries. New ideas do not mean that earlier interpretations were 'wrong' - merely that that was what the available evidence suggested at the time. The greatest thrill in archaeology is that every answer raises a new, unanswerable question.

New sites take a while to work their way through verification, into the records and on to maps, but most of the Preseli sites in our Gazetteer are marked on Ordnance Survey map 145 in the Landranger series, or map 35 in the larger scale Outdoor Leisure series (Welsh place-name spellings are disconcertingly variable). The Gazetteer has been arranged for use in conjuction with OS maps, and directions are given only where we have felt that they will either save a lot of time or indicate a particularly good viewing place. A number of Preseli sites are in or adjacent to Forestries, and harvesting and planting of conifers often results in considerable differences between the appearance of boundaries on the map and what is on the ground. Another hazard is the occasional re-routing of footpaths. All the paths suggested in the Gazetteer have been walked in the year preceding publication, but alterations can be, and are, suddenly made. Sometimes this gives unexpected access to previously inaccessible sites; less often, the reverse happens. Keeping to the Country Code will help to ensure the goodwill of landowners in whose fields so many of the monuments are situated; all enclosed land is somebody's means of livelihood. Mention is made throughout of viewing from road-banks: please keep this to a minimum, using gateways wherever possible. If clambering is unavoidable please use existing water-channels or fox or rat-runs, and avoid any damage to the bank or its flora.

Most of Preseli's prehistoric artifacts are held in Scolton Manor Museum (near Haverfordwest) and Carmarthenshire County Museum (near Carmarthen), but a few are housed in the National Museum in Cardiff, and further afield. Museums frequently change their displays, and lend or borrow each other's material, so enquiries should be made before travelling to see any specific individual object. The holding museum given here may not be displaying every piece at any given time. References made to 'lost' artefacts indicates that their present whereabouts is not on record, not that they have been carelessly mislaid!

Many of the plans, diagrams and drawings have been redrawn by hand solely for this guide-book. In every case the draughtsman of the original has been acknowledged. All unacknowledged illustrations are by the writer.

N.P.F.
February 2001

For the Grandchildren,
whose background this is:

Polly and Mia,
Luke and Mark,
Jasmine, and those who
have not yet arrived.

WOOD

8000 - 4000 BC

The huge climatic episodes which, with hindsight, we appreciate as the end of the most recent ice age, proceeded with astonishing rapidity. Because Preseli was either immediately adjacent to, or actually ridden over by the ice sheets of the last two ice ages, there is no evidence of human life or death from the coldest of times, and it is not until the progressive return of the forests in the aftermath of the last glaciation that there are any signs of human life here. The final pulse of the ice faded about ten thousand years ago, leaving a bitter, rock-strewn tundra lacerated by pounding torrents of glacial meltwaters savage enough to cut great clefts and cwms through the hills (Cwm Gwaun is one such), and littering the slopes with boulders which had been caught up in the under-belly of the ice. Then, from being an inhospitable margin dominated by the great ice sheets still receding into the frozen north, Preseli became an extension of the expanding green forests of the continental south. In and around the forests, the composition of which changed as time elapsed and the climate warmed, came the animals and birds whose habitat was proper to each phase and stage, and with them the small and at first dependent human groups who were a component of the same environmental systems. It is at this stage that we have our first contact with man in the area, but in a landscape and environment quite unfamiliar to us.

With the melting of the ice, a huge weight was lifted off the land, which gradually rose upwards. At the same time the ice was still slowly dissolving so that the sea-level, too, was rising; but the melt water was flowing into world-wide seas, and its effect took longer to culminate than the local re-adjustment of the land. As a result a great plain emerged, reaching far out into what became Cardigan Bay when the sea-level eventually caught up. This rich maritime lowland, stretching from St. David's to the Lleyn Peninsula, was bounded on the east by the uplands which are our present coastal landscapes.

Stag resting in open grassland.

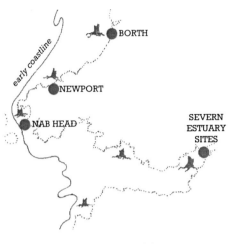

Sites where drowned forests are most frequently visible.

The plain itself is now under the grey waters of Cardigan Bay and these lost woodlands, known as the 'submerged forests', extend out from the coast, a source of myriad legends. The finest exposures are often to be seen at Borth, to the north, and Whitesands Bay, south beyond St. David's; but the fullest 'showings' are unpredictable and may be erased by the activity of the next high tide. At the north and west parts of Newport Bay certain conjunctions of tide and weather cause the covering sands to be gouged out from around ancient tree stumps, and at low tide these can sometimes be seen: fantastical black stumps shrouded in seaweed where once ferns flourished. There must be numerous significant archaeological sites under the modern sand on the modern sea bed; from time to time fine spreads of red-deer antlers have been washed or dredged up, and an antler tine was recovered from the submerged forest under Newport beach. The skull, horn cores and some bones of the extinct wild ox (the aurochs), which can be seen locally in Scolton museum, give some idea of the awesome size and proportions of this magnificent beast.

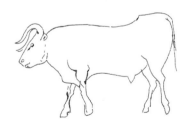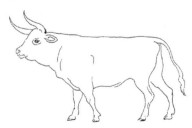

Aurochs Bulls.

Left: *Abbé Breuil's well-known tracing of an Ice Age (Magdalenian) engraving in Teyjat cave, Dordogne (after Bahn, 1998).*

Right: *Outline of the last known life-drawing of an aurochs, from an engraving found in 1827 in a shop in Augsburg. Despite the disparity in technique and skill, the 19th century drawing shows that the wild aurochs was still built for speed and aggression, and proportioned quite differently from modern domestic beef and draught cattle.*

One of the largest aurochs skulls, complete with horn cores, ever found in Britain came from Borth, a mere sixty miles north of Newport. A perforated antler sleeve also found at Borth was originally assigned to the Mesolithic, and published as such, but has since been recognised as Neolithic and dated to 2416 BC.

It was over this plain that human groups hunted and camped, unintentionally leaving behind them the débris that make up the archaeological record. Off Liverpool and in the Severn Estuary, which now also covers a drowned wetland, they left their footprints in the clay - the oldest footprints in Britain, made some time before 5200 BC. The traditional label for the hunting-gathering groups of this period is Mesolithic, or Middle Stone Age, as it comes between the Old Stone Age (Palaeolithic) of our earliest ancestors - the epochs of the great ice ages - and the Neolithic (New Stone Age), when agricultural and settled community life developed. But the Mesolithic is anything but an interim stage between one phase and its successor. It is a five-thousand-year-long success story of extraordinary adaptability, flexibility and adjustment, during which human groups all over Northern Europe contended absolutely successfully with a complete, inexorable change in the flora, fauna, climate, weather and ground-surface as well as land-loss and eventual islandisation.

After the periglacial tundra had given way to the early forests of small softwood birches, hazels and alders, these were in turn succeeded by the large hardwood oaks, elms and ash trees. Spear heads and grooved arrow-shafts which had once been made from bone were now made from abundantly available hardwood; axes and adzes were invented to deal with basic woodwork, and picks to grub up edible tubers and roots. The large flint tools of the Palaeolithic were re-designed as composite tools made of minute pieces of flint worked with a technical skill and mastery of material which is quite

Perforated antler sleeve found at Borth. (After the drawing in Cardiganshire County History, *vol. 1,*

breathtaking. These tiny, geometrically shaped flakes and blades (microliths) were mounted with resin or natural birch pitch in grooved hafts, several in a row, to make up very tough serrated or barbed hunting spear and arrow heads. Equipped with these, a hunter could bring down the largest game.

At Lydstep, near Tenby, a wild pig was found with two microliths, probably part of the weapon which killed it. In the Museum at Scolton there is a magnificent collection of local flints for such tools and weapons, which come from the Mesolithic sites on Nab Head, near St. David's.

Quite small groups of hunter-gatherers appear to have moved around their terrain in patterns and sequences, following the movements of the herds in their quest for appropriate fodder, and at the same time moving to and fro around the natural harvests of seeds, roots, wild honey, berries, nuts, fungi, shellfish and birds. Many sites around Britain indicate that almost exactly the same spot was visited time and again. It is thought that many of these small groups would have joined together for seasonal gatherings, perhaps based on occasions such as the breeding and laying seasons of water-fowl, the rutting season of deer, or the haul-up of seal on the shores. Coastal areas - rich in shell-fish, seal and sea-birds - became very important, and some groups may have spent their whole lives hunting and gathering along the shrinking littoral.

Clustered around the mouth of the Afon Nyfer at Newport are a few sites from which such diagnostic microliths and other worked and chipped flints have been recovered. It may be that these were left by people hunting water fowl at the river margin, or preparing for a foray into the land which then lay beyond to-day's shoreline (there are dug-out canoes dated to this time elsewhere in Britain, and perhaps such were used among the swamps of the lower Nyfer).

In 1922 and 1923 over seventy flint cores and the blades which had been deliberately struck off from them were found in the area of Newport bridge (see *Gazetteer*, p. 67). The flints were lying on the rough stony sub-soil left by the melted ice of the earlier periods, but below the peat which formed as the natural drainage systems of the hinterland were blocked off by the rising sea-level. One of these flint tools was a typically Mesolithic minute blade, with secondary working down one side and part of the second. There was also some artificially chipped felsite and a considerable amount of fairly large lumps of charcoal where the hunting group had prepared their weapons, lit fires for protection from wolves, bears and lynx, and perhaps made myths about reasons for their changing environment. Nearby were three large stones, deliberately dug into the stony level, though these may not have been connected with the chipping floor. Since then a few more blades and flakes have been reported, but the original site has been covered by a dump and by shifting reed-clumps.

There is no need to imagine the Newport Mesolithic as devoid of social verve. Almost anything made of, or painted on, hide or wood is not preserved in our climate and acid soils, but a workshop at Nab Head shows that these people wore ornaments or decorated their garments, tenting or ceremonial staves with perforated shale beads which were produced there by the hundred. Rock-art in Spain seems to show bowmen wearing tufted anklets, garters and curious hairstyles during the chase (perhaps a ritual hunt), and an ambiguously shaped stone from Nab Head figures in the older literature variously as a 'Venus-figurine' or a phallic symbol. However, rumours about its authenticity have more recently circulated, and it is no longer exhibited as a unique example of Mesolithic fancy.

Prehistoric bowman. The curious head-dress and anklets have been interpreted as ceremonial dress; perhaps the action is taking place in a dance-hunt rather than the chase. One of two similarly attired figures in a cave-painting in Cueva Remigia, Spain. Thought to be mesolithic. (After a drawing in Piggott, 1965.)

On the opposite side of Newport bay from the chipping floors, in the damp dip running between Dinas Island and Bryn-henllan, there is a quite different sort of site. Here there are no man-made objects, but analysis of the pollen captured in the layers of peat below the present ground level shows that the closed woodland had been made up of oak, hazel and some birch, with an under-storey of ferns. The little cwm became closed in by thick oak woodland and then, suddenly, the slight hazels and birches grew back in abundance. This could be the result of human interference (by fire or by artificially preserving naturally created openings), followed by a spurt of re-growth of the smaller trees. Some Mesolithic forest-hunters, whose lives were so intimately linked to those of their game, seem to have deliberately kept areas of woodland and forest clear. Once opened, by them or by natural means like lightning-strikes, these spaces would turn to grassland, low shrubs and young tree-growth, all especially attractive to aurochs, deer and wild pig, which would gather in these favoured, artificially produced feeding-grounds. This is not pastoralism, but it is a form of animal management which is a large step away from total dependence on purely natural events in the environment. Interestingly, the peat layer above this interference-level contained a pollen range which could be interpreted as representing a basic level of fodder-supply. Then the phenomena fade, and the woodland appears to have been left untouched for a while.

8000-4000 BC

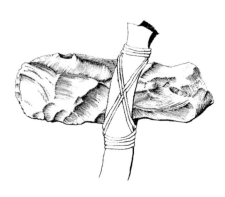

One of the 'tranchet' axes invented to deal with the original wildwood was discovered amongst a number of extensive flint spreads in the area around Llanwnda; another was found just above the coast behind Cerrig y Gof, where the movements of the herds on the plain could be watched from the rich oak and hazel forest edge. An oval stone with an unfinished perforation was found on Bernard's Well Mountain, above what is now Rosebush reservoir. These rounded, holed stones may have been used as 'bola' - stones set along a rope and thrown so as to curl around a hunted animal's legs and bring it down - or as sinkers for fish-traps, but they are generally so well and symmetrically shaped that they are known as 'maceheads', and may have been mounted on a shaft as some sort of ceremonial symbol.

Mesolithic axe. The blades of these 'tranchet' axes are formed by reducing the business-end by cross-wise blows, quite different from the later Neolithic technique. This one comes from Pencaer, just west of Newport, and is in the National Museum. The hafting as usually suggested seems too light for forest clearance.

To the west of the Preselis, near Mathry, excavations at Rhos y Clegyrn (SM 913354) revealed that the daub used in a later house-wall contained a number of Mesolithic flints which must have been either on or in the ground at the time of building. This, like Llanwnda, is a case where exactly the same place was used by Mesolithic groups and the communities who

The hunt. The archer is one of a line of four hunters, into whose arrow-path a stag and six hinds have been driven. This wall-painting in Cueva de los Caballos, in E. Spain, is often used to demonstrate the co-operation and organisation involved in a hunting economy.

(After the drawing in Grahame Clark, 1960)

succeeded them. Mesolithic flintwork now in Scolton Museum was also found in the excavation of the chambered tomb of Carreg Samson (near Mathry, SM 849336). Inland and south of the Preselis there are only scattered indications of Mesolithic activity. A flint microlithic blade was discovered on a site near Glandy Cross (**15**), where the main activities took place in a much later period (but see p. 75), and again at a ritual site of great longevity near Rhosfach (**42**). Mesolithic activity rarely leaves any above-ground traces, and usually only comes to light when a later site in the same place is excavated, so these co-incidences of place may be over-represented.

This is a narrative of 'rocks and stones and trees', because their behaviour and their position in the landscape defined the potential and the limitations of Preseli for the people and animals who came to live among them. Those groups of Mesolithic hunters and gatherers were the base population upon which all subsequent change was visited, and their understanding of the Matter of Rocks, Stones and Trees underpinned the knowledge and experience with which later communities used and abused the land. They lived in our Dreamtime.

This famous antler head-dress was recovered from a Mesolithic settlement at Star Carr, Yorkshire. It has been perforated to accommodate attachments, and the inside smoothed out for comfortable wear. It may have been used as a decoy in the hunt, or as a shaman's head-dress. Since its discovery people have come to see it as a kind of Mesolithic icon. (Drawn from photographs in J.G.D. Clark, 1954.)

8000-4000 BC

EARTH

The Dawn of our Past; 4400-2400BC

Today, for the first time for more than six thousand years, the populations of North Western Europe no longer live on the land they work. The presumption of agriculture, which still underlies so much of our law, diet and disease, social hierarchies and religious festivals, was initiated in the Neolithic, but is no longer valid. The Age of Farming is over; it has become our Past, and its beginning is of peculiar significance.

The conventional term 'Neolithic' (New Stone Age) recognizes that all non-organic tools and weapons, functional and prestige, were still made of stone, as they had been since the beginning; but the thing that was really new was nothing to do with materials. The term 'First Farmers' is now frequently used instead, for the new thing was settlement: the selection of a place in which to breed and feed domestic flocks and herds, and to sow and harvest cereal crops. Subsistence for man and his animals was to be produced artificially *in situ,* and the community must remain in the selected place to complete (and later repeat) the cycle.

The Neolithic era did not just 'begin' as the dot com era has in our time. On the Preseli coast two processes, both natural, had reached a stage which at least inhibited the continuity of western hunter-gatherer life. The great hardwood forests had closed in (reaching much greater altitudes than the present tree-line), and the sea-level had risen, at times with terrifying rapidity, and drowned the grazing lands of the old maritime plain. Into this pressure-pot of stress, economic but no doubt social and psychological as well, came rumours of new ways of managing the environment: stock-raising and planting.

There must have been actual 'first' farmers, and they must have come across the sea bringing domestic cattle and pigs, sheep and goats, and possibly grain seed with them in actual boats - none of the domestic species was native. As well as strange livestock, they brought the techniques of growing, harvesting, storing and milling grain, and the skills of shaping and firing the ceramics which went with their economy. The precedents for their pottery styles and tomb-architecture are in the lower Rhineland and North-West France. Most of our earliest Neolithic sites are near coasts on the south and west of Britain, and on both shores along the length of the Irish Sea, which was only a barrier in foul weather - these immigrants were accomplished seamen. For them the sea was a unifying concourse, far easier and safer to cross than the miles of closed forest of the inlands and uplands.

The Neolithic settlers cleared and burnt their selected places, sowed and reaped and harvested. They foddered, fed and bred their stock, hunted and fished their locality until it was exhausted, and then moved on and did it again next door. Some areas, especially in the highlands, and perhaps including the Preselis, never recovered. The earliest settlements are on light, easily managed soils and gravels and, in some cases, perhaps the areas already opened as Mesolithic game-runs. What happened to the native groups here is a mystery. There are subtle and so far unverifiable hints in the archaeological record that the two populations, even after both were fully agricultural, retained some primal distinction, but the evidence is blurred and fitful. In many instances there may have been no Mesolithic/Neolithic break, merely a transition time when which you were depended on how and where you fed and ate your stock, and the form taken by your origin stories.

Although it is outside the Preseli area proper, the site at Rhos y Clegyrn (SN 913354 - see p. 12), west of Fishguard, is well worth a visit. Only a mile or two from a group of fields where an enormous spread of flints, including Mesolithic microliths, was found, were the remains of some very rare early Neolithic huts which were discovered

Wheats.

Left: *Einkorn, a Neolithic wheat;* Right: *a modern, unbearded wheat.*

beneath a later Bronze Age ceremonial site (the standing stone is still there). The daub (hardened mud or clay) used in the wall of one of the houses incorporated a number of Mesolithic flints, which were probably scooped up accidentally when the daub was being prepared. There seemed to be no evidence of any significant time-lag between the huts, and they were interpreted as perhaps seasonal shelters, something in the nature of wild-fowlers' hunting lodges. Just such hunting was an integral part of the Mesolithic basic subsistence round, but it also supplemented the Neolithic economy, and this is the nearest thing to Neolithic settlement in our area. It is fascinating to see the immigrant groups immediately following the indigenous hunters into the same fowling ground, and then to find that it

4400-2400 BC

became a ceremonial site later still. This continuity of sites is a persistent theme in prehistory, and while it sometimes seems transparently economic to us, it may not have been perceived that way at the time. Taking advantage of interference already created in the woodland must have been far easier than clearing undisturbed forest, and may be part of the reason for the pattern of repeated occupation which took place right along the coastal strip.

Soay sheep were isolated on a Scottish island from ancient times until quite recently. Unaffected by breeding improvements, they appear to be identical to prehistoric sheep. As the photograph shows, they naturally shed their 'coats', which were never developed into fleeces, and do not need shearing.

What the old Mesolithic groups had, and the immigrants needed, was indigenous knowledge. They knew exactly where everything was to be found, and how to get there; who lived where, hunted what and when, and had surplus or need. This may have been the exchangeable commodity which ensured their survival, and possession of it was just as necessary to the incomers as the incomers' tame sheep were to the beleaguered hunters. The impact of this knowledge-network may have been of resounding significance in Preseli. There are possibilities that parts of the all-significant stone axe production and dissemination was in the hands of the native population, whose knowledge of exchange routes and seasons and places of contact was essential to the settlers.

Rocks

Neolithic remains in and around the Preselis fall into two groups: tools to manage the physical habitat, and monuments to manage the spiritual one. Both are made of stone.

If there are no other settlements, there are plenty of stone axes in Preseli. Axes can easily stray from the place where they were originally dropped or discarded in Prehistory, and so do not give an altogether reliable guide to where they were originally used, unless they are excavated from an archaeological site. Flints, because they are less attractive as curios and harder to spot, are much better indicators, but for the same reasons they are found and reported less often. Nonetheless, a number of our axes have been turned up by the plough, and there is a fair chance that this could be where they have lain throughout the millennia. In Preseli, as elsewhere, the majority of the axes, like the Neolithic monuments, are distributed around rather than up on the hills.

Tools

The most familiar Neolithic tools are the stone axeheads. Unfortunately they are not photogenic, but on closer inspection they have much to give. They can, for instance, be horribly sharp. Although many are blunted by use and by the abuses of time, and few are displayed in the museums with the cutting edge facing the viewer, with a certain amount of stooping and peering it is usually possible to see the fine cutting blades on some of them. They come in different shapes and sizes, and in a variety of rock materials. The classic 'English Neolithic axe' of the general literature was made out of flint, but in the north and west, where there are no large flint nodules, such axes are rare and may either have been brought in by their owners, or been the subject of cumulative exchange processes, either in axe form or as raw nodules such as the one found at Fishguard. No less than 'five flint axes with ground blades' were reported in the nineteenth century from near the site of a Neolithic tomb, now destroyed, at Ffynnon Druidion (SN 9236). Unfortunately their present whereabouts is unknown, but the mere fact of such a cache argues for some high-status and successful goings-on in the area.

This axehead, probably Cornish, was found on a beach in South Wales. It was probably washed out of the drowned peat between high and low water mark. Peat is an excellent natural preserver of organic material, and here the axehead was still set in the remains of the Neolithic birch-wood handle. The axe is in the National Museum of Wales, Cardiff. (After Savory, 1971.)

As for size, an unusually large axe, one of a small group of outsize pieces peculiar to Pembrokeshire, was ploughed up near Trellan, north of Llanychaer, immediately above the gorge of Cwm Gwaun; a veritable giant was found at Garnwen, at the south eastern foot of the Preselis, which can be seen in Carmarthenshire County Museum at Abergwili; another came from near Ffynnon Druidion, west of Fishguard, and from Hayscastle, south of Fishguard, came an outsize flint axe - necessarily non-local. Whether these giants were intended as prestige objects or barter specialities, had some peculiar woodworking function or were, even, a symbol of sexual vitality is unclear.

17

Another interesting axe was found near the coast behind Cerrig y Gof, where a Neolithic tool had the blade-end made sharp by a Mesolithic-style cross-blow. Normally the blade-producing flakes were taken off lengthwise - up the body of the axe. Tranchet-sharpened Neolithic axes are most often found with particular tool types, often using bone and antler (occasionally elaborately carved), and accompanied by lavishly decorated pottery. This set of artefacts is common in the east of Britain, but very rarely is any of it represented in Wales (our acid soils would not preserve bone unless it is burned, but the pottery would survive).

While most stone axes come in tones of subdued grey, there is a wonderful piece in Scolton Museum, found not far from Camrose in mid-Pembrokeshire, which is made from a mottled blood and pearl coloured stone from a source at Mount's Bay, near Penzance, in Cornwall, whence axes were distributed as far north as Yorkshire.

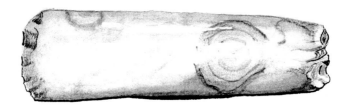

This beautiful flint axehead from Hayscastle, south of Fishguard, may have been part of a gift-exchange or barter system. The circular node, which is so striking now, cannot have been a 'beauty-spot' as it would have been covered by the haft. It can be seen in Tenby Museum.

Normally, western Neolithic stone axes were either made from whatever suitable rock material was available in the vicinity (these are referred to here as 'occasional' axes), or groups of them were made from rock from a specific source where a number were turned out by what have been conceived of as axe 'factories'. The origin of occasional axes can be enigmatic. Many of them were made from glacial erratics which had been dragged hundreds of miles from their source in the stone rubble gripped in glacier moraines, so that what appears to be an axe from a distant source may only have come from a stone in the local river-bed. On the other hand, over thirty different rock types have been identified all over the British Isles and Ireland as producing 'Groups' of products. These Groups have been identified by petrologists and numbered in a special 'Stone Axe Studies' system (Group numbers such as 'Group VIII', sometimes shown on

i.   ii.   iii.

Axe making.

Stage i: *Selected stone has been flaked to the approximate size and shape of the projected axehead. This one is from the Glandy Cross site. (After David & Williams, 1995).*

Stage ii: *The Cumbrian axe from near Brynberian has been ground into its final shape. (After Grimes, 1931.)*

Stage iii: *The complete tool. This hafted axe was preserved in peat on the Isle of Harris, Western Isles. (Drawn from photographs.)*

museum labels, refer to this system). The actual stone-working sites for a very few have been found; the discovery of such a workshop near Glandy Cross makes this one of the outstanding sites of the area. Ironically, since there are no associated structures, there is nothing to see!

From such working-sites hundreds, sometimes thousands of pieces of rock have been been collected, roughly shaped into axe-size form, occasionally finished and then passed on, perhaps for hundreds of miles. This phenomenon has taken on the term 'Axe Trade', but probably indicates gift-exchange systems and other networks as well. The stone used for one Preseli axe, found on the north side of the hills not far from Brynberian, has been identified as originating in Cumbria. The axe is small and not very hard, and may not have been intended as a functional tool.

Two of these rock sources are in the Preselis. One of them, Carn Meini (or Carn Menyn), is the contentious source of the famous 'bluestone' of which parts of Stonehenge are made. Feelings run high on the subject of bluestone, which will be returned to on pp. 47-51. Interestingly, there are comparatively few bluestone (Group XIII) implements in the Preseli area, and none of them is early. The axe workshop near Glandy Cross (see p. 89) used a different

4400-2400 BC

stone, also from the Preseli range - a rhyolite with a wider distribution in South West Wales, known as Group VIII - and there are a number of their products in the area. This rock out-crops at Carn Alw, but no sign of actual quarrying has been found there; many of the axes were probably made from loose erratics trailed southwards by ice to the slopes where the axe-makers found them and set up workshops. Group VIII axes have been found on sites which suggest that they were being made and disseminated for a long period throughout the Neolithic and were used, or at least still valued, in the late Neolithic. Although it is not one of the largest groups, axes and axe parts have been found as far away as Antrim (Ulster), Derbyshire and Norfolk, and there are quite a few flakes and fragments from Avebury in Wiltshire, the greatest complex of Neolithic sites in Britain.

A striking square-sectioned flint chisel from south Pembrokeshire is amongst the Neolithic flints displayed in Carmarthen - an exceptionally precise tool - and an abundance of flint and chert scrapers, borers, knife-blades and *ad hoc* flakes made up the stone tool-kit. There are few flints from Preseli, merely a small collection of scrapers from Ffynone (which probably reflects settlement in the R. Teifi system), a scraper from the north-east side of Foel Drygarn (which might be Neolithic or Bronze Age and which, together with other finds from the vicinity, is most likely to reflect Bronze Age settlement - see p. 45), and a handful of flints from chambered tombs. With one exception, both the monuments and the find-spots lie on the lower ground around the mountains proper, and in the valleys leading into the high land - the selected places of the first farmers. However, wooden and leather equipment, basketry, ropework, fabrics and all the organic objects of which there must have been so much, have not survived. This loss results in the cold and colourless impression of Neolithic daily life which is all that is left to us to display behind glass. The rich inheritance of tactile, musical and aromatic variations of seasonal, geographical and cultural distinctions have all gone.

And then there are the arrowheads. These, too, are contentious. The Neolithic arrowhead was approximately

Neolithic arrowheads.

Left:*The rapidly made hunting and fowling arrowhead.*

Right:*The exquisitely flaked leaf-shaped arrowhead. the very finest of which may have been used in ceremonial killings, sometimes of humans.*

leaf-shaped - laurel-leaf, birch-leaf - and delicately pressure-flaked on both sides. Obviously a missile point. But the prey in which the finest and most exquisitely shaped are repeatedly found embedded is human. Weapons of war? Of ceremony? The other sort of arrowhead is made by breaking a thin flake across and mounting it sideways - not unlike the Mesolithic arrowheads, which were made by snapping a prepared and well-made blade into sections - and these do not seem to have the same morbid associations. Unexpectedly, there are no arrowheads on the hills, only one from the forecourt of Pentre Ifan (**8**).

∗

Pottery was the new skill, the distinctive Neolithic technology. Unfortunately there is very little in the Preseli area, so that it is hard not to read too much into what there is. At Pentre Ifan there was a fragment of a particular sort of pot: hard, burnished, well-fired, sophisticated in shape - not a beginner's effort. Either the bowls of this type, or their potters, originally came from outside the British Isles and Ireland. They are amongst the earliest pot-types known, and seem to be associated particularly with tombs - perhaps for as long as the great megalithic and earthen tombs continued to be built. Other round-bottomed bowls, some with elements of impressed decoration, less severe in shape and often not so well made, may be contemporary domestic ware; the pots from Clegyr Boia in Tenby Museum are of this sort. Together, the two types are usually referred to as 'Neolithic A' or 'Western Neolithic'. The very highly decorated, rather over-done pottery of southern and eastern England filtered into Wales from the east, and was found in an early position at Carreg Coitan Arthur (**4**).

Both domestic and ceremonial Neolithic sites often have pits dug into the ground, and charcoal is frequently found in them. In some of the pits with

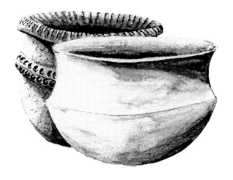

The plain pot in front is of a type now thought to be of special funerary ware found all round the Irish Sea. The shape of this one is like that of a vessel found at Dyffryn Arduduy Portal Dolmen, Merionethshire. (Based on Lynch, 2000).

The decorated pot behind is in a different style and fabric. The tradition from which it comes is proving to be much older than had previously been thought. This drawing is similar to a vessel from the blocking of Gwernvale chambered long-barrow in Breconshire. (Based on Britnell and Savory, 1984.)

burned contents the charcoal perhaps represents burned wooden bowls which may, or may not, be lost versions of the expensive ceramic forms.

Monuments

Most of the monuments of the Preseli Neolithic are the big stone chambered tombs which have exercised a powerful attraction to visitors since time immemorial. Nonetheless, there are enough curious aspects to them to raise the question of whether they are actually tombs (though there is no other useful name for them). One of their most remarkable features is their frontage. The entrance to nearly all types is embellished in some way: by a fore-court, a monumental stone facade, an exaggerated heightening of the front, a passage. Not all these 'entrances' give entry to the burial chambers behind. It may just be that the tombs are something else, and that parts of the privileged dead were buried behind whatever that something was, because of what it was (as in later ages the great and the good might be entombed behind a cathedral altar).

Only a few of the chambered tombs in the Preseli area have been excavated. Many of the remainder are too ruined for their original shape and style to be identified, although representatives of several different types are either obvious, or have been surmised on what evidence is left above ground. Portal Dolmens would seem to have been built around Preseli from about 3500 BC on - the Middle Neolithic, well after the processes of settlement and fusion of communities had shaken down, and when there was a great deal of traffic in goods and ideas.

Essentially a Portal Dolmen is a 'doorway' consisting of two upright stones with a third wedged (sometimes immovably) cross-ways between them to form an H-shape. Roofing these and the small, box-like chamber behind is a capstone, which may be of monumental size and weight, with its heaviest end at the front. The whole was eventually surrounded, but not necessarily covered, by a mound which left at least the top surface of the capstone exposed. Passage-graves are usually in completely-covering round mounds (though the profile of the mound may turn out to have been variable) with a chamber at the end of a long entrance passage. There are several tomb ruins, sadly damaged, which were probably of this type. Both these forms have parallels in North Wales, Ireland and Scotland, whereas the famous long barrows by which the great chambered tombs of the Cotswolds and South Wales were covered may be represented in Preseli by the long mound behind the chamber at Pentre Ifan.

That the chambers were not tombs in our sense is obvious everywhere. The overwhelming majority of deposits are of pieces - sometimes quite small bits - of any given skeleton. Usually a cadaver destined for tomb

Megalithic tomb-types reflected in Preseli.

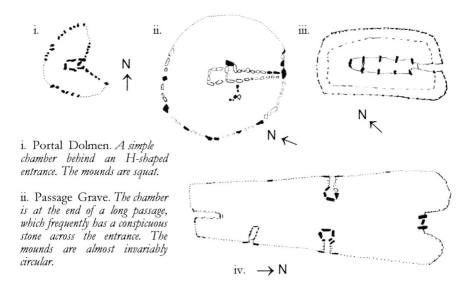

i. Portal Dolmen. *A simple chamber behind an H-shaped entrance. The mounds are squat.*

ii. Passage Grave. *The chamber is at the end of a long passage, which frequently has a conspicuous stone across the entrance. The mounds are almost invariably circular.*

iii. Scottish gallery grave. *Sectioned chambers in variously proportioned rectangular mounds.*

iv. Severn-Cotswold chambered long-barrow. *Side and end chambers are common, and often concealed by walling. This example even has a blind entrance. The trapezoidal mounds can be of inordinate length.*

Drawings loosely based on i. *Dyffryn Ardudwy 1, Merionethshire;* ii. *Satellite tomb Z at Newgrange, Co. Meath;* iii. *Knowe of Yarso, Orkney;* iv. *Belas Knap, Gloucestershire. Not to scale.*

burial seems first to have been exposed (probably on a high platform) so that weather and predators would deflesh the bones; only some of these were then put in the chambers of tombs. Others were kept in alternative significant places, and some perhaps carried around for generations. Whole skeletons are extremely rare. Rites vary from tomb to tomb, and in the same chamber. So far there is no discernible 'Neolithic burial rite', just an impression that the chamber and the apparent entrance to it are not necessarily a unit.

Another known thing - amongst all the unknowns - is that only certain people were represented in the chambers. There are not enough bones for everyone to have had a bit entombed. In most types of tomb there are scarcely any remains; even in the most prolific there are not enough to

4400-2400 BC

reincarnate sufficient people at one time to build it. The fact that the burials were multiple has been taken to indicate a pleasantly egalitarian society, but the organisation involved in tomb building, and the selectivity of bones and body parts included in them, rather undermine this generous view. There may, for example, have been a theocracy controlling the rites. One of the obvious features of most tomb types is inaccessibility from the front; the blank slab at the front of Carreg Coitan Arthur (4) and the closed facade at Pentre Ifan (8) are typical of the evasion of the obvious entrance which is characteristic of chambered tombs (the gaping fronts of some of the tombs to the north of the Preselis would be peculiar anywhere, but are known in Northern Ireland). Side entrances were blocked by drystone walling which could be dismantled and rebuilt, and through such small and undignified gaps the most recent remains were thrust. In many instances the gaps are so small that they suggest that special children may have done the tidying and re-arranging inside. There are children's bones, too.

Formally restricted 'porthole' entrance to Rodmarton chambered tomb, Gloucestershire. (After the drawing reproduced in Crawford, 1929.)

Most tomb entrances face somewhere towards the southern half of the compass, with a preference for south-easterly orientation. There are Irish and Scottish passage-graves definitely constructed so that the mid-winter sun can penetrate into the depths of the chambers - Newgrange and Maes Howe are the most famous - but the orientations of the Preseli tombs are not particularly marked.

*

A great change swept through British Neolithic communities somewhere around 2500 BC. The climate, the *force majeure* of agricultural economy, took a turn for the wetter and cooler; soil degradation and erosion set in. Whether in answer to this or to some other stress factor, settlements were heavily defended, and siege and battle ensued. Carn Ingli is every

Carn Ingli

beleaguered war-lord's dream redoubt. Land, river-systems and sea approaches are all covered from various view-points on the pear-shaped heights of which Carn Ingli itself is the eastern-most summit, a fact well appreciated in the Iron Age and perhaps long before that. Evidence from other parts of the British Isles points to some fairly startling mortuary practices, including possible 'victims' shot sometimes with especially fine arrowheads (the direction of entry of the missile point indicates that they were either strung up or shot from behind whilst lying on the ground). Fatal arrow wounds and many injuries, as well as the ambiguous evidence of burned dwellings, all suggest that agrarian tranquility was, certainly on occasions, breached. It is now widely recognised that by the later Neolithic a number of defensible sites were fortified, such as Crickley Hill in Gloucestershire, which was taken and razed, and Carn Brea, in Cornwall, where c.3000 BC around seven hundred arrowheads were fired at a settlement defended by a sturdy six-foot stone wall. So far there is no direct evidence for belligerence in West Wales, but the settlement at Clegyr Boia, near St. David's, is perched upon a prominent rocky outcrop very similar to that at Carn Brea, and it too may have been similarly defended in Neolithic times. Carn Ingli was extensively occupied during later times, and amongst the remains of numerous huts and enclosures are a some very similar to those at Carn Brea and Clegyr Boia. A defensible position does not necessarily imply a defensive structure; the current perception is that the west was less heavily settled than the east of Britain, that communities were smaller, familial rather than tribal, and that Wales was predominantly peaceful. However, like Carn Brea and Clegyr Boia, Carn Ingli is seaward of an area which figured prominently in the exchange routes, and it is at least thinkable that from about 2500 BC onwards it just may have played some rôle, if not a pivotal one, in the politics of the Preseli area and its resources.

At about this time new forms of ritual monuments emerged, different ways of making and decorating pottery became dominant, new stone-tool sources were developed, well settled areas were abandoned and new ones opened up, and the great communal tombs were closed up and sealed, as if there were something inherent in the rites themselves which demanded closure. Not all of these changes and accompanying unease are actually demonstrated in the Preselis, but there are hints here and there which reflect most of it. Generations before the 'Neolithic' (in the strict sense of stone-tool using) yielded to the succeeding metal-inspired epochs, some of the essential tenets of Neolithic life had already given way.

Pentre Ifan chambered tomb

SKY

Monuments

Henge and Cursus Monuments

Around 2500 BC certain non-physical aspects of Neolithic life underwent a dramatic change of direction. The results of this were to have a profound effect on Preseli and eventually bring the area to some sort of ceremonial primacy in south-west Wales. Although basic Neolithic economics remained much the same, religious and social development fractured. The generations living at this time seem to have gone through a period of accelerated social evolution, perhaps even crisis. It is impossible to tell whether it was an exciting and invigorating time, or one bedevilled by want and fear. The somewhat cooler, drier summers and colder winters which set in might well have affected the Preseli uplands, where the potential for tree growth and regeneration was always slight, and undoubtedly this would have added to the sense of flux felt by these generations, with increase in open grasslands for grazing and simultaneously a possible problem with erosion on existing crop-growing areas. The look of the increasingly open land around them may well have left the Neolithic communities (whose origins lay in forest clearings) susceptible to the new open-air rituals spreading from the north, where the differences in day and night length are most extreme and where phenomena like the aurora are most frequent.

Many of the central themes of Neolithic culture had, in effect, run their course. Stone and mound-covered communal burials ceased to be made, and the great tombs like Pentre Ifan were sealed. Collective burial ceased, and individualised funerary practices became statements of personal rank, consistent with a hierarchical social context. The concepts of chiefdoms and individual power-holders are often seen as appropriate to a religion based on observation of the sun and moon and their apparent 'control' of seasonal events. The institution of a single war-lord and/or priest, who dictates the (necessarily seasonal) activities of all the members of his society, appears to some anthropologists to reflect celestial organisation.

Of the earliest monuments connected with this new direction in spiritual affairs, the henges are the best known. Castell Garw (**135**), a circular earthwork at Glandy Cross, was thought to be a possible henge and is suggested as such in the literature. Recent exploration, however, has indicated that it is no older than the Late Bronze Age. Another site at Pantymenyn, to the east of Glandy Cross (see p. 87), is a possible candidate, although it, too, is thought more likely to be a denuded settlement. There remains Preseli's most eccentric monument, the rectangular stone setting of

Bedd Arthur (**97**). High on the hills directly across the saddle from Carn Meini, it is unlike anything else. However, Early Bronze Age studies have recognised a rectilinear theme in ritual and ceremonial sites, with a possible origin in rectangular Neolithic mounds, and Bedd Arthur may be a henge-like expression of this. Unlike a henge, however, it is extremely high up, although it is close to the crossing of the east-west and north-south trackways, and henges are frequently sited close to routeways.

Three and a half miles (5½km) south of Glandy Cross, aerial photography has revealed a possible Cursus at Llandissilio (**103**). It cannot be seen on the ground, was discovered only a few years ago, and has not been confirmed by excavation. A Cursus is exactly the opposite of a henge in shape: a long, thin, straight 'course' lined by precisely parallel banks. The two monument types seem to have been built at the same time, and often quite close to each other. That both may owe their origins to some facet of the pre-Neolithic, indigenous culture is a possibility; the significant part played by the native communities in the development of Preseli is a recurrent theme.

It is only very recently that any pieces of the type of pottery connected with henges (Grooved Ware, still sometimes called called Rinyo-Clacton ware) has been found in Preseli. These vessels are flat-bottomed, decorated with geometric sets of incised grooves, and still attractive to the modern eye. Until a few years ago Grooved Ware was thought not to have reached Wales at all, but recent excavations have discovered a quantity of it at huge henges in the Marches, whither both henges and Grooved Ware spread from east of the Severn. Small pieces (sherds) of pottery with the same sort of decoration were excavated a few years ago at Carreg Coitan Arthur tomb(**4**). This style possibly originated as far north as the Orkneys, where there is one of the earliest henges yet known, and where the built-in stone dressers and shelves in houses like those at Skara Brae would seem to call for flat rather than round-bottomed pots! One Scottish pot was found to have a residue of a native hallucinogenic herb. As Grooved Ware soon appeared all over

Grooved Ware pottery is curiously rare in Wales, although it is overwhelmingly abundant in much of Britain. This example comes from East Anglia. (Based on Piggott, 1954.)

Scotland and England, perhaps the naughty herbal tea played some part in its success.

*

Preseli might seem to lie on a trade-route between Ireland and Wessex, two regions where the production of early metal objects and their acquisition dominated the centuries between 2300 and 1500 BC. The ridgeways that cross the hills present a land-route over the peninsular of south-west Wales which avoids an unpredictable sea-route between the cliffs and currents around St. David's. Whether this was significant in the days of the intrepid mariners of the Late Neolithic and Early Bronze Age is debatable. Preseli may not only have been on a trade-route; it may have been a destination.

To us, the transition from dull stone to sharp and shining metal blades would seem to be one of those discoveries which jerk prehistory towards modernity with less of a giant step than an Olympic long-jump. But it may not have been that way. Copper-smelting had been known in Europe for centuries before anyone took it up in Britain or Ireland. The technique spread from the Near East, and was probably discovered through the inclusion of ore in potters' firing hearths; most of Europe went through a long Copper Age which is only fleetingly represented in these islands. To begin with, Irish objects, styles and techniques were the first to reach Wales. Metal analysis is sorting out those Welsh axes which physically came from Ireland from those made from Welsh copper and subsequently bronze. Parts of North and Mid-Wales are rich in metal ores, and in the last decade it has been generally (but not universally) accepted that a number of copper-mines were opened early in the Bronze Age (the best known is on the Great Orme Head, Llandudno, and is open to the public).

All over Northern Europe the last centuries of the third millennium were distinguished by the presence of something best described as a cult. This is the Beaker Culture, which used to be thought to represent a migration of a people with a distinct raft of possessions which were buried with their dead. The most familiar are the 'beaker' itself (an expertly crafted and often very beautiful drinking-vessel), novel archers' tanged arrowheads and stone 'wrist-guards', and copper and bronze tools. Individuals were buried alone under small round barrows, usually in a foetal crouch, with grave-goods appropriate to gender - all very different from previous practice.

From about the same time, the centuries around 2300 BC, copper axes start to turn up as chance finds outside graves. This is important, because the connexion between the introduction of metal-working and the introduction of the Beaker Culture is not clear-cut. They seem to have happened at about the same time, but there is no evidence for actually

29

attributing them to the same real-life persons. The much stronger flat-axes made of bronze (a mixture of copper with tin) almost immediately succeeded the pure copper ones, and do seem to have been genuine tools, whereas the pure copper ones may have had more arcane functions. Four flat-axes have been discovered in Preseli; three of them were found not far from the Taf valley, the fourth below the north slope of Foel Drygarn, at the head of the Nevern river system. On present evidence it seems that flat-axes in Britain may have been made by native metal-workers, not by immigrants, and the significance of this in Preseli is that stone battle-axes were made at the same time, also by native stone-workers.

There are several of these extraordinary weapons - if such they were - made of Preseli bluestone. One one of them was found in a Beaker barrow at Wilsford, near Stonehenge. Bluestone was also used to make traditional axeheads, which have been found as far apart as Monmouthshire, Devon and Suffolk. Specifically Early Bronze Age tools made of bluestone include axe-hammers (large dual-purpose hafted tools) which turned up in Shropshire and Essex; an adze was found in Sussex and a macehead in Devon. As might be expected, bluestone axe-hammers and battle-axes occur in Wales, several close to the Preseli area (see p. 48). The only Preseli sites which have yielded Beaker pottery so far, are Carreg Coitan Arthur chambered tomb (**4**) and the Parc Maen complex at Rhosfach (**42**). In neither case were the Beaker sherds germane to the original construction of the monument;

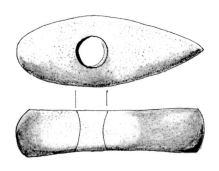

Battle-axe made of Preseli bluestone. It was found in a bowl-barrow on Salisbury Plain (Wilsford G.54) with a copper or bronze dagger, and is thought to have accompanied the later of two burials, the earlier being accompanied by sherds from three different Beaker vessels, and six arrowheads. It has unusually severe lines

and at Parc Maen, at least, the pottery from which the fragment came was locally but expertly made. The emerging picture is not of a Preseli invaded, dominated or even infiltrated by the original bearers of the Beaker cult, but of a lively native community with a tradition of stone-working and far-flung contacts which now brought it in touch with the strange, copper-hungry groups from the continent.

Preseli became somewhere very special in the Early Bronze Age. The great ridgeway track along the hill-tops, the north-south ridgeway running down towards Milford Haven, and the slopes and valleys between them are stamped with monuments to Bronze Age ceremonial and funerary ritual. Within our area there are a number of ceremonial sites of considerable significance: nearly fifty confirmed standing stones, single or in pairs; numerous large boulders of which the status is unclear, and nearly seventy known (and a further fifty possible) funerary barrows. It is a remarkable concentration, one of a number of such richly endowed areas up and down the British Isles and Ireland which were identified as enhanced or enhancing for some reason no longer known to us. The mood of our time would suggest that metal trade-routes (such as those from Ireland and Wessex, where the Early Bronze Age literally had a golden age) or resources such, perhaps, as bluestone might have given rise to Preseli's flowering. Alternatively, the small farming communities which here were predominantly stock- rather than grain-based were for this reason particularly well-placed to convert to a formal Bronze Age society headed by a cattle-rich warrior elite with individual power vested in material possessions. Equally, it may be that something quite unrecordable, something numinous or psycho-phenomenal, contemporary or already tapped by the ancestral communities, branded the area as spiritually significant; even that the spiritual was the perceived reason for material success.

The Early Bronze Age is one of the most glamorous periods of pre-history, and the people living in Preseli between about 2200 and 1500 BC controlled one of the most elaborate ritual centres in western Britain at the time. Visually, the most striking monument is the circle at Meini Gwyr. This has been reconstructed by the Dyfed Archaeological Trust, and stands at the heart of the great funerary complex at Glandy Cross (**56**). Beside it two of the stones of Yr Allor are still standing. This may once have been a tomb, but may have been a 'Cove' - rare and enigmatic rectangular monuments whose function is unknown. Around them, the now-domesticated landscape of sloping pasture is puckered with burial mounds. The hill-top ridgeway is crowned along its whole length with formidable stone cairns. Standing stones, solitary or in pairs, mark precise spots of unknown significance, and the stone circle at Gors Fawr crouches under the shadow of Carn Meini. All these and much more which is less visible, many sites still undisturbed, stand as relic witnesses to a time and place of great moment.

*

Stone circles
One result of closing the great megalithic tombs was the disappearance of a focal setting for the remains of the significant dead. Many henges and later ring-monuments have cremated or inhumed remains carefully incorporated

into them, although they were not primarily burial-places. Only a minute proportion of the living merited a lasting interment, whether in ritual monuments or in purpose-built burial cairns or mounds. In many cases the two functions are no longer obviously separable, perhaps because the rites concerning both mortal and after-lives may have remained closely interwoven. The idea of human sacrifice has always sent a dubious quiver up the spines of the living (the slightest hint of it immediately brings the media circling around the dullest of post-holes), and there are indeed some rather odd burials in and around post and stone circles, but no more than have been found in any pre-modern period.

The inspiration which had turned people's minds from the underground to the celestial, and produced the henges, very soon elaborated on the simple earth circle. Pit circles and post circles were constructed within henges or newly erected as complete monuments and almost immediately standing stones and stone circles made their appearance.

Wales is not one of the parts of these islands rich in stone circles, and Pembrokeshire has unexpectedly few. Although there is now no verified henge in Preseli, there are two or three sites representing the development of circular monuments. The stone circle at Meini Gwyr (see pp. 87-9), which is set on a circular earthwork with a single entrance, is an example of the 'embanked stone circles' that have much in common both with the henges which came before them, and with the free-standing stone circles built somewhat later, often within an existing henge (Stonehenge itself is the most famous example). Meini Gwyr is dated to about 2000 BC, by

Photograph: Ailinor Evans

Gors Fawr Stone Circle

which time the new systems of ritual and burial were well in place. At Letterston, about fourteen miles west of Meini Gwyr, another embanked stone circle often recorded as Letterston 'Henge' was subsumed into such a ritual and burial site. There is now only one free-standing stone circle in Preseli, near the source of the Eastern Cleddau at Gors Fawr, Mynachlog-ddu. As such circles go, Gors Fawr (**100**) is a small and rather dumpy example, similar in this way to those in the South-West of England and Ireland which some see as later than huge circles like Marden or Durrington Walls in Wiltshire. The smaller, lower circles like Gors Fawr are sometimes held to have a more direct connexion with funerary practices than the large henge-replacing ones. It is unknown if any burials are associated with the Gors Fawr circle.

Gors Fawr has been somewhat spoiled in recent years by the growth of large clumps of gorse amongst and close to the stones. Earlier photographs and postcards of the site show how much more visible and impressive it was before this was allowed to happen. A description from 1911 reports that 'there are also traces of at least one avenue', but nothing corresponding to this has since been observed.

It has been suggested that some of the enormous monoliths grounded near Tafarn y Bwlch may be the remains of a stone circle. If so, it would have been extraordinarily large and impressive, and some record, if only in name or story, might be expected; however, nothing has been identified.

Rings & ring-cairns

Ring-cairns, as opposed to the other circle-monuments, are actually burial places. The typical image of an Early Bronze Age burial mound is of a round stone or grassy 'tump', but in fact there are many varieties and shapes of these round barrows, and the ring-cairn is an extreme example (see p. 34). Here the 'tump' element has been left out altogether, only a 3D plan of its outside, as it were, being built. The result is a structural ring with an empty circle inside it, often slightly raised. Impressive boulders were sometimes used to line either the inside or outside of the ring, and where there are entrances the whole structure seems to incorporate elements of henge, circle and barrow building.

The dead are usually represented in ring-cairns either by their ashes (often only a token amount) or by the ashes and charcoal of their funeral pyres. Cremation requires intense heat, and pyre-charcoal is almost always oak. The inner circles, used for rituals, were sometimes paved and sometimes trodden as if by circle-dancing; sometimes posts were set up. A wealth of music, odours and ceremonial activity is represented by the beaten earth,

Cairn and barrow types found in Preseli

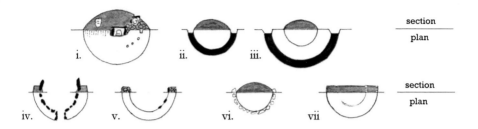

i. *Cairn (stone built) or barrow (earth mound) showing central primary urn cremation in a stone cist and arc of post-holes, both dug into the old ground surface under the mound. Later secondary urn cremations, one in a cist, are shown higher up, dug into the mound itself.*
ii. *Bowl-barrow. The earth from the ditch has been used to build the mound.*
iii. *Bell-barrow. A space (berm) has been left between the ditch and the mound.*
iv. *Embanked stone circle, not primarily a funerary monument.*
v. *A ring-cairn, a genuine funerary monument.*
vi. *Kerb cairn, with mound embellished with a ring of boulders.*
vii. *Platform cairn, showing internal circle which may not be structural.*

Features dug into the old ground surface and covered by the mound may be part of the same funerary rites, or much earlier than the mound. Those dug in from the surface of the mound may be much later.

silted-up holes and scanty, cold ashes. Once such a site had been built and established it attracted subsequent burials, and some continued to be used for centuries, either as ring-cairns or re-designed, often by covering the entire ring with a large cairn or barrow which in its turn received further, later burials.

There are ring cairns by the path below Foel Drygarn, at Glandy Cross and perhaps at Eithbedd, but the most visible are Carn Enoch (**20**) and Glyn Gath (**21**), on the east slopes of Mynydd Dinas. They are both much dilapidated, but strangely atmospheric.

Between Henry's Moat and Eithbedd the large cairn called Dyffryn Syfynwy Stones or Dyffryn Circle (**33**) is in fact a large barrow with twelve tall stones around and against it, some still upright. It has not been excavated, but the relationship of the stones to the mound is so immediate that it is more likely to be a burial mound with a magnificent surround than a stone circle that was ever free-standing.

Dyffryn Syfynwy 'Circle'.

This was probably once the most magnificent burial site in the area. Much of the barrow has eroded away, leaving the monumental kerb of upright stones looking like a stone circle.

Round barrows

Despite the many divergent forms of burial-mound, most Early Bronze Age notables throughout Britain and Ireland were buried under some form of round barrow or cairn. Both sexes and all ages are represented: the aged, the damaged, the new-born. Some form of caste-system, whether temporal or spiritual or both, must have ordered this selection. Here in Preseli, where the soils are very acidic, bone is not preserved, and well-cremated ashes leave little scope for analysis; but there is no reason to think that the selective processes practised elsewhere were not also operating here. Nothing, however, has ever emerged to suggest what those processes were.

Barrow Cemeteries

Sometimes a number of barrows are found grouped together in what appear to be cemeteries. In some places there seems to be a principal barrow around which others gathered; elsewhere, as at Crugiau Cemaes (**34**), north of Eglwyswru, no distinction is apparent. A spectacularly large barrow cemetery developed at Glandy Cross (**56**) incorporating a number of different mound-shapes including one ring-cairn, with two other possibles, two or three flat-topped mounds, and five or perhaps six platform cairns (like filled-in ring-cairns). Nothing has yet emerged to indicate whether cemeteries like Glandy Cross were reserved for local burials, or whether some other qualification entitled significant dead from elsewhere to be brought for burial in these centres. There is intriguing evidence from other funerary complexes in Wales that some remains have been buried twice, at two different locations.

2500-1400 BC

Cemeteries of this kind were used and added to over many centuries, and individual barrows were used, redesigned and re-used over great periods of time. Here at Glandy Cross, Goodwin's Row barrow (see pp. 89-91) is a striking example of this longevity. The persistent use of white quartz in barrows such as this is a theme running right through the history of burial mounds in the Neolithic and Early Bronze Ages, and the time-consuming labour of collecting it is a comment on the strength of the conventions. There is no evidence yet to show what the connexion between the dead in any individual barrow may have been - whether kinship or relationship depending on some non-physical ranking like membership of a guild, priesthood or cadre governing funerary rites.

Tragically, the few prehistoric objects found in the nineteenth century in the Glandy Cross area have all been lost. As recorded, they are an interesting collection, for they date from the period in which the majority of the barrows were probably built, down to the time when a dagger or sword and a Late Bronze Age axe were lost, perhaps by travellers passing through the now-deserted cemetery. The oldest pieces in the vanished collection were pottery, including two funerary urns; one of these was smashed in front of the discoverer's eyes when a horse tripped over and broke it, scattering whitened bone and ashes, and the other turned up when the present road was being built. Two pottery beads thought to be Bronze Age were discovered in a garden at or near Goodwin's Row.

The remaining two pieces are little cups, the pygmy cups or Accessory Vessels of museum shelves. These tiny pots are usually quite lavishly decorated but not always well-made, which suggests that each one was designed for use at a specific funeral and never intended to last in the temporal world. Many of them have either small holes in their sides, or cut-out designs, and they used to be called incense cups, as they would make excellent censers. The burning of aromatic herbs and gums at funerals has an honorable history; however, it now appears that both alcohol and cannabis had a part in certain Bronze Age Mysteries, responsibility for their introduction being currently laid at the feet of the Beaker-bearers. The positioning of the little holes in many of the pygmy cups now suggests an alternative way of using them (though it may be a while before we have a museum label saying 'Bronze-Age Bongs'). Pygmy cups from neighbouring areas can be seen in both Carmarthenshire and Scolton museums.

Many barrow cemeteries either developed from or were built amongst other types of monument, and the relationship between these is unclear. Glandy Cross cemetery is almost surrounded by standing stones, but as these seem not to be directly funerary, their presence must refer to some other aspect of this immediate place or its relationship to the wider landscape. Early records and descriptions suggest that several fine

36

Curious things.

Pygmy cups were made in a wide variety of shapes. Shown here are:

Centre: *A cup found near Llangyndeyrn, Carmarthenshire, in a collared urn with a cremation and an Irish-type dagger.*

Right: *An elaborately decorated example from Glamorganshire.*

Left: *Window-like panes cut in an example from a rich barrow-burial on Salisbury Plain. One of the cups once found near Meini Gwyr was described by Fenton as 'like a miniature Stonehenge', and may have been something like this.*

Below: *Patterns on the bases of pygmy cups. Centre and right are below the cups they decorate. The design on the left is from a vessel similar in shape, but more highly decorated than that from Llangyndeyrn, and probably comes from Ceredigion.*

Above: *One of a pair of gold Bronze Age discs from Tedavnet, Co. Monaghan. A number of such pairs of discs have been found in Ireland, some in England, and a few similar pieces on the Continent. The design is remarkably like that on the base of the Llangyndeyrn pygmy cup, and is often interpreted as a sun-symbol, indicative of sun-worship; it could also be a wheel-symbol - or neither! The other two base patterns are among the many which may be variations on the theme.*

The cups are all between 2-3 ins high; the disc is 5½ ins across. All the designs shown are complete. Left: Devizes Museum; drawing based on Annable & Simpson, 1964; Centre: Sketch made in Carmarthenshire Museum; Right: National Museum of Wales; based on Savory, 1980; Disc: National Museum of Ireland; based on a photograph in Cone, 1977.

---

monuments and other sites have been demolished in the last two centuries as the land has been brought into modern use. One of the most intriguing of these lost monuments, very close to Meini Gwyr, seems to have been a 'cove'; these are fairly rare features, made of upright stones set on three sides of a square, the most famous of which is probably at Avebury.

Sky-line barrows

High above the barrow-cemetery, marching along the hill-tops to the north, are the massive stone cairns on the east-west ridgeway. There can be little doubt that they were intended to be visible in exactly this way. These are, in effect, 'the tombs of princes'. The largest of them seem to occur in small groups, four on the Frenni Fawr, three on Foel Drygarn, and so on. Absolutely nothing is known about the relationship between the groups or between the barrows within each group. Seen from the ridgeway from Foel Drygarn to Cerrig Lladron, the hill-tops show themselves as a linear series of peaks far more obviously than they do from below, and the massive cairns seem to be sited in direct response to the contours. Some of the much smaller cairns and barrows which lie on and near the route are now almost invisible, even when the gorse and heather are at their lowest.

It is these smaller, and probably later barrows lower down which, standing as they then did largely in unenclosed scrub or rough pasture, have yielded more accidental information, perhaps because they were less obviously tempting to early treasure-hunters (Roman legionaries, for example, left a scatter of small losses along the ridgeway where early investigators record that several cairns had already been disturbed, and an actual coin dated to AD 69 turned up with urns, bone and ashes in one of the four barrows at Crugiau Cemaes). Near Llanychaer the destruction of a barrow for land-improvement resulted in the discovery of a fine-quality urn with cremated bone in a cist apparently approached by a passage. Near Llangolman new fencing revealed an urn, also with bones, and a separate cremation came from the same district. From the Taf side at Hebron, just north-east of Glandy Cross, another urn, four cremations and an 'earthenware pot' seem to have sadly been lost. Several urns from the same reaches of the Taf were discarded in the nineteenth century on the curious grounds that they were Roman, and another set of two or three were discovered near Tegryn during collection of hard-core for road repairs. All these 'urns' come from the later stages of the Early and Middle Bronze Age, and may have been secondary burials in existing barrows - in most cases there is not enough recorded evidence to tell. The urns themselves vary in details of shape and decoration, and one of the most surprising things about them is the great variety of size; some are reasonable pots but others are astonishingly large and, it must be admitted, ill-made and unattractive - to the extent that they exert a perverse appeal all of their own. Another surprise lies in the disproportionately small size of the bases. This has led to the belief that they were purpose-made for burial, and indeed they are often found upside-down, to which position they definitely appear most suited. However, now that sherds of such urns have been found in domestic settlements this presumption has been withdrawn (on the other

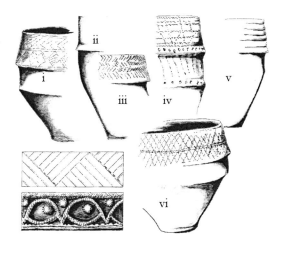

Bronze Age funerary urns.

i & vi: *From Croesmihangel barrow. Both were found upside-down in cists, and may have been primary burials. (Based on photographs in Nye, Harrison and Savory, 1983.)*

ii: *Shape indicated by sherds in Goodwin's Row barrow, found containing a male cremation and oak charcoal, in a little cist dug into the top of the mound. (Based on Murphy, 1990.)*

iii: *Here the overlap of the herring-bone design has not lined up. Top of an urn found with burnt bones in a cist under a cairn near Fishguard. (After Grimes, 1939.)*

iv: *Suggestions of lattice patterns overlie the simpler design made with twisted cord on this urn buried after the building of the cairn at Parc Maen. (Based on Marshall, 1991.)*

v. *Rilled decoration on the collar of an urn from Cross Hands, just east of A. Taf. (After Grimes, 1939.)*

Panel. Top: *'Infilled triangles' - one of the commonest motifs.* Below: *Rare raised design on an 'encrusted urn' from North Ceredigion. (After Grimes, 1939, and sketches made in Ceredigion County Museum.)*

hand they must have been made somewhere, and perhaps the domestic sherds merely reflect the presence of a mortuary potter). Domestic sites of this period are so rare that no generalisations can be made about what, or even whether, pottery was much used.

After about 1400 BC most burials do not seem to have called for the inauguration of a fresh barrow; instead, inurned cremations, sometimes several, were carefully dug into existing monuments of all varieties. At Croesmihangel barrow (**48**), under Foel Drygarn, this happened twice. The cairn site at Parc Maen (**42**), near Rhosfach, enjoyed an even longer history, perhaps being returned to for nearly a millennium. There a cairn was constructed over and around a standing stone and burial, and numbers of small holes or pits, some filled with pure oak charcoal, were dug beside it. Remains of three urns and a magnificent Early Bronze Age flint knife (plano-convex type) probably came from secondary urn burials in the cairn, and two more exceptional pots, one of them the Beaker-type vessel mentioned above (p. 30), were buried nearby. Finally, perhaps around 1300 BC, a much later style of jar was put into the cairn or its surrounds.

2500-1400 BC

Standing stones

The tall grey stones rising out of moorland and field are the most obvious of all Preseli's prehistoric monuments. There are nearly forty sites where single stones, pairs or even rows of standing stones are still *in situ*, and as many again where single stones might be fallen monoliths or where records indicate that there was once a standing stone. Only about a third of the certain standing stones are approachable, and while more can be seen from roads and tracks, many are well inside the boundaries of private land and are not accessible.

Mynachlog-ddu stone pair with Carn Meini in the background.

The stones have always exercised a strong attraction, not least because their origins and purpose are unknown, and they have stood open to each generation's interpretation (including that of 'confounded nuisance' to the plough!). Archaeologically, they are usually referred to as earlier Bronze Age, and pending more focused excavation it still looks as if the majority may have been erected at some time during the centuries between 2200 and 1400. However, where they have been included in modern excavations, there are signs that some, at least, may have been raised in Neolithic contexts, and that the stones visible to-day are not a coherent group but part of a tradition which spanned a thousand years, and which may have changed its emphasis during that time. Earlier antiquarians and tourists assigned them to 'Druidical practices'; the more pragmatic generations, having disposed of the Druids, saw them as way-markers or territorial boundary markers; the astrologically inclined interpreted them as seasonal or astral markers. In fact there is no evidence to show that they were any of these things. They just stand there. Some of them, certainly, attracted burials and others appear to commemorate ancient activities, the non-material aspects of which are inaccessible to us. What was it about that particular porched Bronze-Age round-house at Stackpole, on the south coast, or the wild-fowlers' huts at Rhos y Clegyrn, that inspired the raising of stones over their ruins - sites which remained ritually operative for a further thousand years?

Statistical analysis of the positioning of single, paired and rows of stones in Pembrokeshire has suggested that while the rows are upland, single stones are most frequently erected in valley or lowland areas, with the pairs somewhere between the two. This led to the corollary that the single stones might be the earlier as a type, and the multiple arrangements followed the progress of land-utilisation on to the highlands. Recent analysis of Irish standing stones has come down heavily in favour of personal monuments, a tradition originating well back in the Neolithic and possibly accounting for their presence in, and in front of, tombs (the felled stone beneath Pentre Ifan comes to mind). Other Irish work on paired stones has suggested that the exact covering of one stone by the shadow of its pair is replicated within minutes by separate pairs, and may not just denote an agricultural season but a particular moment of a particular day. However, it must be said that so many stones have been removed over the centuries, so many prostrate stones may or may not be fallen standing stones, and so many rather lumpish boulders may have qualified as standing stones, that a true record is a wished-for, not an attainable ideal.

Tools and weapons

Halberds
At some point in the Early Bronze Age someone lost or hid a weapon-blade just beside the river at Brynberian. It is made of copper, about the size of a large dagger, but very slightly and assymmetrically curved. This is the blade of a halberd, a striking weapon mounted at right-angles to the shaft, rare in England but well-known in Ireland and Wales.

Because halberds continued to be made of copper, long after bronze had proved its superiority, it is likely that the halberds in these islands are not weapons but insignia. Exquisite miniature halberds less than 4cms long,

Halberds

i. *The Brynberian halberd (now in Scolton Museum). The three rivet holes for attachment have corroded away.*

i.

ii.

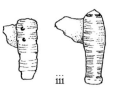

ii. *Warriors raising halberds as if they were gleaming pennants rather than weapons. It looks as if some Bronze Age fighting-men went into combat naked, as did some Greeks and Celts after them.*

iii

iii. *Pendants (under 3½ inches long) in the shape of miniature halberds, buried with warriors on Salisbury Plain. Left: The blade is copper or bronze; the shaft is amber, bound with four strips of incised sheet gold. Right: The blade is bronze, and the whole shaft incised sheet gold. Both are in Devizes Museum.*

> i. *After Grimes, 1951, and sketches made in Scolton.*
> ii. *From a North Italian rock-painting reproduced in Savory, 1980.*
> iii. *After Annable and Simpson, 1964.*

with shafts made of incised sheet gold and amber bound with gold strips, were buried as personal adornments in the richest of the Early Bronze Age warrior graves in Wessex. There are rock-pictures of halberds being carried as if in battle (because of the angle at which they were mounted, the wounds they would have inflicted are horrible to contemplate - like the pecking of a monstrous raven), but they are not part of the standard warrior equipment. The Brynberian halberd must be looked upon as something from a very rarified and aristocratic context.

The gold which enriched the great warrior tombs of Wessex is, in Britain, an earlier Bronze Age phenomenon. Very recent work in the well-known Roman gold-mines at Dolau Cothi, in Carmarthenshire, indicate that gold may have been extracted there in the Bronze Age. There is a pair of gold cuffs from the neighbouring Llandeilo area which may have been actually of local Welsh gold. It would have been in full knowledge of these extraordinarily rich and stratified societies that the great cairns and ceremonial centres were raised in Preseli.

Battle-axes

Perhaps the most enigmatic of the Early Bronze Age weapons is the stone battle-axe. These are barbarous objects, the larger ones are enormously heavy, with an appalling crushing-power, and even the smaller ones would smash a brain-pan, a spine or a joint with a single blow. Continental evidence suggests that they were indeed used in battle, but whether as parade symbols of terror or actually swung in wrath is unclear. There are so many of them that it seems fearfully likely that they were really accoutrements. A bluestone battle-axe, now in Carmarthenshire Museum, was found near Trelech, and another on the hillside above Pentre Galar, not far from the site of two robbed and destroyed round barrows; interestingly, a third was found near Llanboidy in the Taf drainage area, which may have been a water-way, as was a macehead (see below). None of these others was made of bluestone, and they all vary in stone-type and shape.

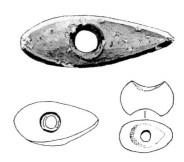

Above: *Trelech battle-axe, made of Preseli bluestone. (After Wheeler, 1925.)*

Below. Left: *Outline of a bluestone axe-hammer from Merionethshire;* Right: *A later curvaceous battle-axe from Wiltshire. Axe-hammers are larger, wider and usually less carefully made than battle-axes. Function has exaggerated divergence from the related basic shapes.*

Maceheads

Bluestone was also used for what are known as 'maceheads'. These are problematic objects with a near-central hole and no blade, coming in every rank from things which might almost be digging-sticks, to the most breath-taking emblems of office in the canon of North European prehistoric stonework. The Cilgwyn macehead (now in Scolton Museum) is unfortunately chipped on one side, and is less regularly shaped than the finest examples, but is still a nice piece. It was turned up by the plough on

Left: *The white Maes-mawr macehead from North Wales, seen from the side. It is now in the National Museum of Wales. The 'accordion' carving on these rare maceheads is also found on earlier antler examples.*
Right: *The Cilgwyn macehead (now in Scolton Museum), seen from above, is small, dark and simple by comparison, but they must have been endowed with the same significance. (After Grimes, 1939, and Savory, 1962-4.)*

2500-1400 BC

the hill above Cilgwyn, and nothing is known about why it was there or for how long. A couple of hundred yards away some dismantled and scattered stones mark what may have been a chambered tomb (7). It is not impossible that the macehead may have come from whatever that site was, as a number of maceheads of this type have been found in chambered tombs.

The finest macehead ever seen comes from the great passage-grave at Knowth, on the Boyne, in eastern Ireland. Carved with spirals in relief and intricate cut-out lattices, it is a masterpiece in tricolour flint of milk, honey and conker tones. The same lattices were carved on the pure white Maesmore macehead found near Corwen in North Wales, but again this magnificent object was not associated with anything that might yield information about how it came there. The Cilgwyn macehead, as a humbler member of this family of rare and wonderful objects, must have had considerable significance in the community which possessed it.

Part of another bluestone macehead, now in the British Museum, was found near Sidmouth, in Devon, one of a number of bluestone objects from the south of England. Maceheads are frequently recovered broken, perhaps in parallel with the death of their possessor.

Part of a quartzite macehead of a slightly different, possibly earlier shape, was found in a stream-bed at Velindre, quite close to Cilgwyn but the other side of Pentre Ifan. It is now in Scolton Museum. Another came from near the river at Llanboidy, less than a mile downstream from the battle-axe. The flint knives known as 'plano-convex' (or, less courteously, 'slug'), which in this part of Wales sometimes accompany urn burials, also have a native cultural history, some of which they seem to share with the maceheads. The only one of these very distinctive and wonderfully-made knives so far found in Preseli was in an urn at Parc Maen (42). A complete one from Rhyndaston, not far from Scolton, can be seen in the museum there, with the pygmy cups and cremations and the urns which held them.

Work-day tools

Secular and mundane activities still depended on the use of stone. The most frequently represented tool around Preseli is the axe-hammer. This is a heavy-duty, multi-purpose workhorse of a tool, holed to take a strong haft, with one blade end and one hammering end. The Preseli ones all come from the lower ground below the mountains: from the fertile land north of Eglwyswrw, from the lower land south-east of Glandy Cross, from south of Efailwen, from near Hebron by the Taf, and two from Llanfyrnach. One of the Llanfyrnach axe-hammers and one from north Cardiganshire are made of bluestone as, perhaps surprisingly, are axe-hammers found in Anglesey and Shropshire,

Essex and Wiltshire. On the face of it, they do seem rather large and mundane tools to carry or present to sites so far from Preseli. This will be discussed further, later on (see pp. 47-51). A maul or hammer from near Mynachlog-ddu, two perforated stones from Llanfyrnach and a perforated disc from near Eglwyswrw could all be Bronze Age.

There are two Bronze Age flint scrapers from Cilgwyn (perhaps used in leather or hide preparation) in Tenby Museum, and another from below the north slope of Foel Drygarn, close to where both a flat-axe and the lost axe-hammer were found, suggesting that there may have been Bronze Age settlement here or on the hill above (see p. 30). Another collection of flints picked up on a bluff between two streams east of Boncath includes eight scrapers of two different sorts and a long flake, and might represent hunting activity either in the Bronze Age or Neolithic.

Despite the hundreds of people who walk the Preselis every year, no Bronze Age or Neolithic hunting arrowheads have ever been reported. Environmental evidence gives every indication that the hills were sparsely wooded, if not fairly open throughout most of the first centuries of the Bronze Age, when hunting remained an integral part of the economy, and the absence of arrowheads is slightly surprising.

Palstaves

By about 1500 BC, the bronze palstave axe had become Tool of the Day. As techniques developed the shape of palstaves changed, and the two from Preseli, which can be seen in Scolton Museum, differ in detail. The Pentre Ifan palstave is probably the earlier of the two, and was found on the edge of the 'shelf' on

Bronze axes from Preseli.

Above: *Flat axe from Llanfyrnach (see p.44), found in potato drills in 1841 and now in Carmarthenshire Museum. (After Griffiths, 1893, and photographs.)*

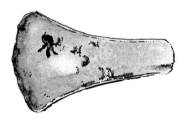

Below: *Palstave from near Pentre Ifan, found near a spearhead when 'blasting stones in a field'. Now in Scolton Museum. (After Savory, 1947.)*

2500-1400 BC

which the tomb was built, some distance from it to the east. The single rib down the centre of the blade is a style usually adopted by smiths from the east of Wales. The Boncath palstave, however, has a hafting loop on the side, an improvement common in later types, and was brought up accidentally during ploughing. Carmarthenshire Museum has a number of flat-axes, palstaves and socketed axes set in modern hafts showing how they must have looked when in use.

Technically, the palstave was a great advance on the flat axe. The latter was made by pouring molten metal into a single shaped stone mould and, when cool, refined by hammering. The early palstave is essentially a flat-axe with the sides hammered upwards into flanges, and a device half way down the face to prevent the blade from driving back up into the haft. As the design became more sophisticated, so did the metal composition become more standardised, and the casting technique more demanding. This resulted in the development of the bi-valve mould; here half the longitudinal shape of the palstave was cut out of either part of a pair of stone moulds which were bound together during casting. The molten alloy was poured into the whole palstave-shaped space between them, and the two halves separated when the metal had cooled. The casting seams where the stones had originally met are often quite visible despite the subsequent trimming and smoothing.

The details of Bronze Age metal combinations and casting techniques have been extensively studied, and North Welsh bronze-smiths were amongst the most innovative and prolific in Britain. This may have been stimulated by the presence of ores in North Wales, where the awesome Great Orme Copper Mines, if they really are of this period, demonstrate a level of social organisation and continuous labour-availability equalling that required for any building at Stonehenge. Away from the mines travelling smiths carried both stocks of ready-made implements and raw material around among the locations where they worked, rather as some farriers do to-day.

Daily life
Just west of Maenclochog a particular sort of field-system perceived beneath the modern agricultural patterns is possibly Bronze Age (32), but otherwise there are few remains in Preseli of the settlements and farms of the later Bronze Age. Only 'burnt mounds' and some clearance cairns may show where people actually worked on the land, and both these stone-heap remains are infamously hard to date. Elsewhere plough-marks and field-systems are now well known all over Britain and Ireland, but actual dwellings associated with them have everywhere proved elusive. The few that have come to light in Wales show that both plank-built and post and panel type round-houses were used. Environmental evidence shows that uplands, including the Preselis, were cleared and grazed more extensively in

this period than at any other time before or since. Unable to support this, the thin soils quickly eroded and degraded and the process of peat formation began, to give the Preselis exactly that 'wild and natural' beauty with which the Bronze Age pastoral farmers have endowed us.

STONEHENGE

Over eighty bluestones were used at Stonehenge. It was there that they were shaped and dressed, and quantities of the resulting chippings have been found. They were used perhaps three times, two arrangements being dismantled and rebuilt, and one of them incorporating fine architectural features, perhaps smaller versions of the massive sarsen trilithons still standing. Finally they were arranged as a horse-shoe and a circle, both dwarfed by the colossal sarsen settings between which they were re-erected.

The Preseli hills were recognised as the source of the bluestone as early as 1923. In 1956 the late Richard Atkinson described in *Stonehenge* how individual bluestone blocks could be rafted along water routes across the Severn Estuary from Milford Haven to the mouth of the Avon at Bristol. A bluestone axehead (now in the National Museum of Wales) was found at

Caerwent, near Newport, which (unless it was a Roman soldier's souvenir) shows that carriers of Preseli goods passed along the Welsh shore; and a bluestone boulder which may have come from a long-barrow lies very close to the second section of Atkinson's waterway route. As recently as 1999 Sean McGrail, the leading expert on prehistoric craft, expressed complete confidence in Early Bronze Age boatmen's ability to transport the four-ton stones destined for Stonehenge on a tri-maran canoe formation, using the Severn tides and currents for impulsion and a minimum of paddlers for navigation. The question of how it was done is not a problem - only whether it was done.

There is nothing, either at Stonehenge or in the Preselis, to suggest any reason for a bonding of special places. At home, in Preseli, bluestone is used sparsely in the monuments (although a comprehensive petrological survey has yet to be made). There is nothing to indicate that it was a preferred or special stone here. The tools and weapons made of bluestone are not numerous; indeed, it is among the less used resources, far outranked by the local stones used earlier in the Neolithic. The distribution of *objects* made of bluestone is wide, and loosely similar to that covered by the infinitely more numerous Craig Lwyd axes from North Wales. Although it was used for prestige objects - maces and battle-axes - there are twice as many working tools, axeheads and axe-hammers (although individual axeheads may have had both functional and prestige value). In fact, were it not for its architectural use at Stonehenge, bluestone would appear to have no more significance than many another suitable and attractive local stone.

There are, and always were, a number of scholars who doubt that the bluestones ever were brought from Preseli to Wiltshire. The journey is simply too long, too difficult and, on the face of it, too unreasonable. There must, it is felt, have been another source of bluestone. Either they came from a so far unidentified outcrop closer to Salisbury Plain, or they were brought there by glacial action. The directions in which the glaciers of the last glaciations flowed have been thoroughly studied, but no known flow could indisputably have brought them from Pembrokeshire to Salisbury Plain. Erratics found on Steep Holme Island in the Bristol Channel turned out not to be bluestone after all, and no other bluestone, in block or pebble form, which would indicate such glacial action, has yet been found. It is almost impossible to believe that there were only ever exactly that number of exotic stones lying around in a group, which were all picked up and used for their rarity value. Moreover, there is no known source of bluestone anywhere but in the few outcrops in the Preseli hills. However, the feeling is that neither the study of erratics nor the search for alternative outcrops has yet achieved sufficient depth to dismiss the possibility that the bluestones may have come to Salisbury Plain either by natural means, or from elsewhere - perhaps nearer, or perhaps somewhere compatible with known glacial direction. Most of today's authorities treat the subject of the source of the bluestone with careful reserve. There are two other stones at Stonehenge with apparent sources in the Milford Haven area, and the arguments for and against glacial transport apply equally to them. The curious occurrence of a bluestone boulder recorded as coming from the spine of Bowls Barrow near Stonehenge - a long barrow constructed generations before the bluestone settings - did seem to weigh in favour of the 'erratic' theory; however, doubt has now been shed on whether the stone in question is the Bowls Barrow bluestone. It just might have been a bluestone brought from Stonehenge. The arguments are far from resolved, and the matter is unsettled, but there still may be that small bluestone boulder astray and as archaeologically explosive as a loose cannon.

That the bluestones were special is unquestioned. Two important changes have developed in Stonehenge studies. First, the monument is increasingly seen as an indigenous development not inspired from outside (by, for example, Beaker Culture over-lords or theocrats), but evolving from within the religious and social context of the native late Neolithic. The other change is that the dating of the various phases of Stonehenge has been reassessed. Both these developments reflect back upon the Preseli connexion.

Here in Preseli the monument at Meini Gwyr and either the dissemination or the possession of the new copper flat axes show the emergence of a successful native community on and around the watershed between the Taf and the E. Cleddau. It is improbable that this community and the local native community which began developing the Stonehenge area in the same way were not in contact with each other. The evolution of both was in line with similar emerging centres in other special places around Britain and Ireland. It does not presume any unique connexion between these two in particular.

There is a further enigma. The distribution of the bluestone objects in southern England has already been referred to. It is an intriguing fact that this distribution is as appropriate to a source in southern England as to one here in Preseli. The same distribution map could be read to show either a single source in either area, or two quite independent small sources, both using an attractive but otherwise insignificant locally available stone. Two sources could only be proved by the discovery of two manufacturing sites, a discovery not yet made. If the significance was in the stone itself, then was it the geological composition which mattered, or the landscape from which it came? There is nothing obvious in the composition of the stone; it is attractive, but those who possessed the truly beautiful jadeite axes made in Brittany were not provoked to ship hunks of north-west France across the Channel.

So are we looking at the transference of a special or sacred landscape epitomised by the stones? Had the concept of moving landscapes been learned by those whose life-sustaining tools and weapons had always been made of stone? On a small scale, the movement of stone away from its outcrops must have been familiar: outcrop to scree, to river, even as far as to the sea. Stone can, and does, move. It is not improbable that origin-stories and migration-myths may have incorporated memories of the catastrophic changes in environment which had so affected the later Mesolithic population - tales of moving seas and moving lands (the perennial Atlantis myths are a contemporary echo of this). The contribution of these older, indigenous groups to many aspects of what had seemed typically 'Neolithic' activities is increasingly seen as highly significant - a lapsed viewpoint current in the sixties, and now reviving. At a more immediate level, the ebb and flux of forest and wildwood caused by the interaction of clearance, regeneration and natural erosion in unnaturally cleared areas (such as highland) would have added to an overall consciousness of an inconstant landscape.

Could we then look at the Wiltshire bluestone as a 'removed place'? Not as eighty-two stones brought from Preseli, but as Preseli itself brought to Wiltshire by the descendants of the stone-working caste? What is there at Carn Meini and the other outcrops to indicate that it was in some way special? A recent study of human environments suggests that the highest stone on the Carn Meini bluestone outcrop was deliberately set there to enhance the significance of the site; in short, that *this* bluestone *was* moved, albeit not very far, for a non-functional purpose. The same study considers the possible significance of the polishing of stone, and the special rocks and boulders on which the tools were polished (both active and passive participants in the same activity), as having super-functional connotations; and in 1986 a possible polishing-stone was recorded at Carn Meini.

Corrugated earthfast stone at Carn Meini; natural weathering, or the result of ritualised polishing activities?

Above: *Plan of the sarsen trilithons (black) and the Phase IIIb bluestone oval at Stonehenge, about 1540 BC. Some of the bluestones were subsequently removed to make the oval into the famous 'horseshoe', or open rectangle. (After RCHME, 1979.)*

Below: *Bedd Arthur from the same angle.*

Immediately opposite Carn Meini is the rectangular hengiform monument of Bedd Arthur (**97**). This stone setting is absolutely undated; however, musings on the shapes of the ground-plans of the early bluestone setting and the trilithon setting at Stonehenge might prove provocative. There are also a handful of quarrying sites around the outcrop at Carn Meini, and the remains of what may be a few circular huts. Unfortunately it is not possible to date any of these. Bluestone weathers into blocks ideally suited to monumental masonry, and has been used as such in the historic period, as indeed it is now. The indicators of activity around Carn Meini could belong to any age later than, but including, the Late Neolithic.

All in all, it has to be said that there is no clear indicator, let alone evidence, that the Preseli bluestone outcrops had any non-physical or physical significance whatever in the Late Neolithic that might account for their removal to Salisbury Plain.

STONEHENGE

WATER

1400 BC-AD 56

The Clouds Gather

Some time before about 1000 BC a long-term rainy season set in, which was to last for approximately the next six hundred years. All of Britain and Ireland were deeply disturbed by its effects, and the Preselis, facing the incoming rain clouds, suffered irretrievably. Already, such tree cover as there ever was had long been cleared, the uplands grazed (some think to denudation point), and their pastures turned into the blanket heather moorland for which they are so greatly loved to-day. But perhaps the most profound effect may have been on the spiritual life of the generations living through the onset of this climatic change. Water took on a new significance - an element, perhaps, to be appeased.

Suddenly the archaeological record falters. It falters because people no longer buried their dead in permanent monuments. With a few notable exceptions, this is true of most of Britain right through the Late Bronze Age and the Iron Age. It is thought that instead of interring the ashes of the dead, these were scattered or deposited in water - lakes, rivers, swamps. After a few late depositions of cremations in existing barrows such as Croesmihangel and Parc Maen, and the discarding of a few sherds of Middle Bronze Age pottery at Meini Gwyr, there are few signs of life or death in Preseli during these grey centuries.

What little there is, however, reveals a very different social complexion. This is best interpreted as defence of the best land and the diminishing returns from it under threatening conditions, as is known to have happened elsewhere between 900 and 700 BC.

Carn Ingli outcrop

The hillfort is built on the crag and its skirting shelves and slopes. The open moorland around the west and north sides is strewn with the remains of huts and field boundaries.

Although only Castell Henllys, near Newport, has been excavated in recent enough times to provide reliable evidence, it has been suggested that the first defences there and at Carn Ingli may have been wooden fortifications, erected some time before the construction of the Iron Age stone ramparts. There are two areas of field-system on the south side of Carn Ingli which are considered to be of Bronze Age type, and a similar phenomenon has been recorded high on Mynydd Dinas, near Carn Enoch, but it is almost impossible to date field-systems with any certainty.

At the other end of Preseli from Carn Ingli a cache of broken weapons was buried deep in a pit near the source of the Pedran stream. The Pant y maen hoard was discovered in the 1860s when the boggy ground was being drained, and some of it can be seen in Carmarthenshire Museum. In all, one sword, one sword-handle and two pieces of sword-blade, a piece of a rapier, a scabbard chape, portions of at least a dozen spearheads and fragments of ferrules, and two bronze rings had been bundled up together and hidden in a deep hole some time in the Late Bronze Age - just when things were beginning to look really bad. The emphasis on spears rather

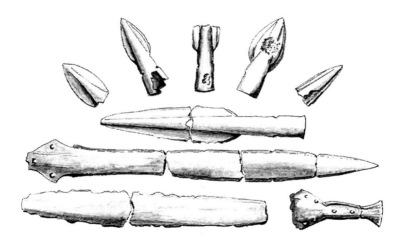

The Pant y maen hoard

A few of the thirty pieces found in 1859 in a pit in peat. The large spearhead (shown horizontally here), another small spearhead and a ferrule can be seen in Carmarthenshire Museum. The broken sword blade and the sword handle at the bottom may not belong together. The handle would have had bone or wood panels rivetted on either side of the metal plate. The weapons were broken up with hammer blows as well as breaks and bends. (After Griffiths, 1956-8.)

1400 BC - AD56

than swords is typical of western Britain in the later Bronze Age, and an early account of this hoard mentions that some of the ferrules still held part of the 'oaken' shaft. While a variety of woods have been identified in spear sockets, ash is the most usual, with oak next. Ash naturally produces straight supple branches, especially when pollarded, and the much-hymned Welsh ash-groves may well have had a bloody origin.

All the larger items in the hoard had been broken into pieces of a similar length so that the whole collection could be bundled up for storage and carrying, and also re-smelted together. 'Founder's hoards' like this are the smith's collection of used weapon-quality scrap, from which he would make fresh arms, free of the hazards of incipient cracks, metal-fatigue, loosening rivets or any other life-threatening fault, and perhaps in an updated style. Significantly, all the pieces were from weapons - no axes, chisels or other tools. This may indicate that the special relationship between chieftain and smith, which continued right through the succeeding ages into Early Christian times in the west, had already been forged.

Another spearhead with a leaf-shaped blade was found in the same area near Pentre Ifan as the palstave mentioned above (p. 45), and may be a little earlier than those in the hoard. A sword and 'two pots' were found at Meini Gwyr, and a socketed axe either with them or near by, but these have sadly been lost.

The casting of later Bronze Age weapons and tools was more demanding than that of the solid palstaves. The bi-valve method was elaborated for items like spearheads, but for the socketed axes, where the ratio of solid blade-end to empty hafting space was very different, the technique known as 'lost wax' or *cire perdue* was developed. Here a clay core, representing the wooden haft, was enclosed by a wax model of the axe to be produced, and the whole enveloped in a clay case. When fired the wax would run off, leaving an axe-shaped space into which the molten bronze was poured. The solidified axe was then released by breaking the clay mould.

A socketed axe

By this time lead, as well as tin, was being added to copper to produce a more tractable metal, and some very magnificent and elaborately decorated panoply was made - marvellously (if impractically thin) decorated shields like one found some sixty miles north of Preseli in Cardiganshire, and huge bronze feasting cauldrons which eventually found their way into western mythology *via* sacred water shrines in the bogs and rivers in which they were regularly deposited. The beautiful three-metal alloy remained the material for fine and luxury items for many centuries, but after about 700 BC the realities of battle and subsistence began to be expresssed in cold, hard iron.

'The Coming of the Celts'?

The 'Celts' of today's idealisation didn't come, they were there already. What came were climatic, demographic and cultural pressures which were felt all over Europe from the Czech Republic to Connacht, and which produced similar social and cultural responses amongst European populations which had never been particularly separate. Portable goods carry with them the artistic context of their place of origin, and the 'Celtic world' was neither a political nor an ethnic one, but a stage of European-ness evolved in response to a mutual history on one hand, and increasing pressure by expansionist classical civilisations on the other. One of the effects Roman conquests had was to break up that casual, unformalised European-ness. When the Empire eventually collapsed, lots of little 'countries' and 'peoples' were left with identities and histories which had been variously affected by whether they had been inside the Empire or outside it, or trading with it, or ignored by it. In Britain, only half of which had been inside the Empire, the base population and those areas least affected or unaffected by Rome came with hindsight to be seen as especially 'Celtic' in an ethnic way which would have had no reality in the Iron Age.

At about the time when the palisades were being erected around hill-top sites, 800-600 BC, something completely new and different happens to the archaeological record. We have speech - we have language. The Celtic which underlies both the Irish-Scottish and Welsh-British languages seems to have spread throughout much of Europe from a base somewhere in the east German/Austrian area at some time between 1200 and 800 BC. Latin, too, came from the same original source, and other branches spread east as well as west. By the time the earliest palisade defenses were going up, the Celtic language was taking over; by the time the hillforts were being founded in Preseli, the orders were being given in a Celtic tongue.

The face on this bronze torc terminal from Courtisoirs (Marne) would be recognizable as 'Celtic' anywhere in Europe. Typically 'Celtic', too, is the way the head slyly metamorphoses from unmistakably human at the top to undeniably cervine at the end. (After Filip, 1960.)

Daily life

For once the site record, usually so overwhelmingly concerned with ritual and death, is teeming if not with life, at least with the farms and homes of the living. There are literally dozens of sites all over the lower Preselis, ranging from small single huts to sprawling collections which can best be called hamlets if not villages, and from elaborately defended enclosures to open settlements. Because these were built over many generations, and in differing local political and environmental circumstances, they are inevitably all different. Each one responds to the immediate needs of the founder and the immediate topography of his patch, and so they can only be grouped into very crude general categories of site type.

At the lower end of the scale there are the single round huts, few of which can be said with assurance to be 'prehistoric' in the strict sense of pre-Roman Iron Age (nobody suddenly stopped sleeping in a *round* house just because some scarlet-skirted Roman general had clapped Caratacus in chains). Aside from these isolated huts there are numbers of round-house foundations set amid walls and field-systems which are the remains of the settlements of the pastoral system upon which Celtic Iron Age society depended. The most visible is at Waun Clyn Coch (**130**), tucked under the mountains near Glynsaithmaen. Others, like those on Carn Ingli and Waun Fawr, are less easy to find, especially in summer when they become quite submerged beneath heather and bracken, or are so fragmented by time that they best seen from the air, like those at Craig Talfynydd! Nonetheless, these round houses were the source of the wealth and man-power which, accumulating further up the hierarchy, ultimately made possible the life-style of the élite which sustained the artists, craftsmen and song-makers whom we so revere today.

More substantial than a slave or bondman shepherd's hut (Celtic society embraced both these classes) are a number of these small circular defended enclosures which consist of one or two round-houses within a bank and/or ditch. To us such defensiveness would suggest that times were violent, but what is known of Celtic culture indicates that local violence (cattle-raiding and individual combat) was structured and predicated, so a handsome defense-work might be as much culturally inspired as a response to actual physical threat - perhaps functioning as an expression of status. There are a number of such sites in Preseli, hard to distinguish in function from small hillforts or high-status enclosures defended on all sides. None of them has yet been investigated in modern times, and whether they are really a 'type', perhaps prevalent at a particular time, or a continuous rational use of a defensible spot is not certain.

It is in the second and first centuries BC that the defended farm enclosures are thought to dominate Preseli. Just south of our area, at

Llanychaer enclosure (117) seen from the road, across the river

Llawhaden, serious defence works were revetted on both inner and outer faces, and spectacular entrances involved placements for the display of battle-trophies. (one thinks particularly of the six decapitated heads which probably adorned the gate to the Bredon hillfort in the Marches.) Inside, behind the defences, were round houses and raised storage cells. The store-houses are known as 'four-posters' because the floor was raised off the ground on a platform resting on four posts. This gave some protection from ground damp and from vermin, and is common in Iron Age sites all over Britain. Both these types of building have been permanently reconstructed at Castell Henllys precisely as they stood in the Iron Age, and to stand inside them is a sobering experience.

In high-status sites, it is likely that the stock remained outside the enclosures, and that the interior was given over to the pursuits of which echoes sound in Celtic stories: high living and the acquisition of the means thereof. Analysis of the parts of grain preserved suggest that the muddy end of farming took place at smaller farms, and that the four-posters stored crops brought in, perhaps as tribute. There is evidence, too, for bronze-working, which was a high-ranking craft. The implications are that the elaboration of defence works may have been a statement of rank rather than a necessary precaution against siege or mayhem.

Forts

Amongst the defended enclosures, but also reaching up into the Preselis, and on steeper and more topographically complex land, are a number of promontory forts. There is a general impression - no more, for none of them is well dated - that these were occupied both a little earlier than the lower enclosures and perhaps, at times of genuine unrest, as an alternative

1400 BC - AD56

to them. Chronologically the single (univallate) defended hill-sites are considered to be the earliest, followed by the double or multi-ramparted hill-sites, after which there seems to have been a move away from the hilltops on to lower gound and into defended enclosures. Some of these are really very small, like Tregynon (**118**), above the Gwaun, where a massive ditch and bank cut off an elfin enclosure on the edge of a precipice. Enshrouded now in a beautiful wood, it has an almost fairy-like atmosphere, but as a defended location it seems little short of panic-stricken. Others, such as Castell Mawr (**125**), still have impressive ramparts

Rock-cut ditch in Tycanol wood

but enclose areas big enough to accommodate family units. Another promontory fort on the edge of Tycanol wood (**127**), near Pentre Ifan, encloses an area of approximately eighty by fifty metres, with the interior divided by walling and the entrance actually cut into the rock.

In quite a few cases promontory forts, like enclosures, come in pairs, presumably the result of 'partible inheritance' which ensured equal distribution of land and goods. One result of this was a proliferation of high-ranking fighting-men, represented in the archaeological record as a proliferation of impressively fortified sites, and in story by tales of formalised personal combat and cattle-rustling. Such formalisation was intended to ensure the emergence of the next warrior chieftain with the least cost to lesser men and the land (for although the stories revel in accounts of blood let and thatch burned, that was the purpose of praise-singing). Unfortunately, in Preseli and Wales generally, the acid soils do not generally preserve unburned bone, so there is no archaeological record of the part played by animals, which is such a feature of Celtic art and (albeit derived) story.

The major hillforts in Preseli are undated and largely unexcavated in any modern sense. Elsewhere in Wales there is a perceptible development of fortified sites from the Late Bronze Age on: sites recurrently occupied and refurbished. A few Preseli sites like Castell Henllys (near Eglwyswrw - **123**), Caer, Bayvil (north-west of Nevern - **121**), and Castell Garw (near Glandy Cross - **135**) hint at re-occupation, for early palisades have been found beneath Iron Age defences. It is therefore theoretically possible that the hillforts may also have had a long history. Possible occupation of Carn Ingli in both Neolithic and Late Bronze Age times has already been mentioned, but these are suggestions based on the shape of surviving remains, and such remains are notoriously perfidious.

A general impression of two separate surges of hillfort defence works has been suggested, but we have no idea what particular contingencies these phases may have been addressing. Foel Drygarn and Carn Ingli, although set back from the coast, both command quite astonishing views of the coastal waters. Trade with the Mediterranean world, along the Atlantic sea-ways, expanded from the fourth century BC onwards, and the occupants of the coastal forts may have had some connexion with this, though whether as participants, pirates or potential victims is unknown. The arrival of 'wonderful things' like the Cerrig-y-Druidion hanging bowl in North Wales or the (possibly live) Barbary ape in Co. Armagh are famous examples. Preseli stood in the line of the route of very prestigious objects, and must have been aware of it, even if jealously and at a distance.

Foel Drygarn (**132**) and Carn Ingli (**108**) are the most impressive of the Preseli hillforts. Below Foel Drygarn the defences at Carn Alw (**133**), and below Carn Ingli the smaller fort of Carn Ffoi (**110**) present curious difficulties of relationship. Above the Nyfer, at Castell Henllys (**123**), continuing excavations have produced a number of unexpected results. Here, as at Carn Alw, the entrance was protected by a *chevaux de frise* - one of those

Chevaux de frise *at Carn Alw*

The curving boundaries of the two bands of upright stones show up clearly to the left of the boulder-lined approach. (The enclosure in the left foreground is a recent sheep-pen made of Iron Age defence material.)

1400 BC - AD56

nasty belts of small upright stones set to break the ankles of any fast-moving invader. Since these are not common defence works, it is intriguing that there are two examples in such a small area. This leads to the speculation that a mobile hillfort architect rather than a mere follower of fashion may have been resposible for their construction. Castell Henllys has proved to have a very long history of occupation. It was strengthened repeatedly and imaginatively. Slingshot, the burning of the entrance, and the wicked *chevaux de frise* tell of adrenalin-rich exploits far removed from the loom and the sheepskin bed. One cannot help but suggest that most Iron Age village reconstructions do tend to omit the very aggressiveness upon which the Celts themselves set so much store. There can be no doubt that cattle-rustling across the hills by night must have been the most enormous fun, and that formalised combat must have thrilled arteries pulsing with mead and meat-juice, albeit always on the edge of tragedy. As Cúchulainn put it, when he killed his foster-brother for a gorgeous brooch, 'It was all play, all sport,/ until Ferdia came to the ford' (*The Táin*, trans. Thomas Kinsella, 1969).

Late in the Iron Age there does seem to have been a movement away from the hillforts down to the enclosures on lower and more fertile land. This, coming at about the time when the climate was recovering from the Late Bronze Age deterioration, may reflect an expansion as well as a movement of the population. At a number of places sites are found in pairs, as at the Penybenglog forts (**124-6**), above the Gwaun. This is thought to be due to the Celtic system of dividing inheritance, but even allowing for this, and for the short-lived nature of many sites, the impression is of a period of comparative recovery and prosperity, fortified by such details as the wooden ploughshares preserved in a water-logged ditch at Walesland Rath, just west of Preseli, and the timber settings around one of the Llawhaden house hearths, which may have had to do with roasting spits. (At one Scottish site the remains of no less than two hundred and sixty-six plant species indicate a wealth of possible dyes, medicines, foodstuffs, and magic potions - all to be found in the stories and there demonstrated by excavation.)

Goods and chattels
The repertoire of portable objects found in Preseli is grievously meagre. Some of this is due to the fact that Wales was largely a-ceramic in the Iron Age, and perishable wood and leather containers have not survived to replace the plethora of pots and sherds of earlier times. Iron was such a valuable commodity and its collection, smelting and forging so laborious that none was thrown away, each piece being saved for re-cycling; and since grave-goods were only committed with certain cadavers at rare times and in restricted localities which did not generally include West Wales, any prestige

pieces current in Preseli have disappeared as well.

It is disappointing that the most Celt-conscious district in Britain should be virtually devoid of Iron Age art. There are a few pieces of pottery from one or two settlements (including Castell Henllys) but they are small and frankly rather dull: sherds of mass-made stamped vessels from pottery-using areas on the Marches, whose contents would be of more interest than the ceramics. A quern found at Newport Rectory and then lost may have been either Iron Age or Roman (once the rotary quern replaced the saddle-quern only the rare decorated piece is datable); the unfinished top half of another,

Stone spindle-whorl from the Llawhaden area, decorated in late Iron Age style.

(After Williams & Mytum, 1998.)

to which an equally vague date applies, was found at Coynant, near Llanboidy. If they are Iron Age they do at least confirm bread-making, as the spindle-whorls from Carn Alw and Dinas Island suggest spinning, at those particular places. The Carn Alw spindle-whorl is also unfortunately lost, but it was said to have been decorated with concentric circles and cross-lines - perhaps something like one of those recovered from the Llawhaden sites - which may say much about the status of the woman for whom it was made.

Hillforts in West Wales are notoriously empty of chattels, and it is lucky that the early exploration of Foel Drygarn recovered two splendid stone vessels, recorded as lamps, which are now exhibited in Tenby museum. Interestingly, they are round-bottomed and, as the excavator pointed out, would only stay upright on a soft surface. This seems risky with an open-wicked oil-lamp, and there was a lot of charcoal about. A small jet ring and a few scraps of line-incised pottery speak of contacts with the Marches and north-east England, perhaps in several stages, but the most evocative pieces are glass beads. Two small ones were made of very dark blue glass, and there was a fragment of a yellow one embodying a clear spiral.

Stone 'cup' found on Foel Drygarn, more likely intended for holding molten metal than lamp-oil. (After Baring-Gould et al, 1900.)

The finds from Foel Drygarn are exhibited as a collection in Tenby Museum.

In the Iron Age glass beads were expensive jewellry items, most of them made in Glastonbury and exchanged over great distances, and it has been suggested that one of the functions hillforts fulfilled was the distribution of prestige pieces through the medium of hierarchical gift-giving. Rather pathetically, seven of the Foel Drygarn beads, made of a pale-green glass, were halves, as if such bright personal ornaments were hard to come by and precious even when broken. One had in fact been mended with some sort of adhesive, and it may be that they were of great sentimental value. Either way, they come from a very human and recognisable world.

Glass beads
from Foel Drygarn.

Centre *(and repeated):* Yellow glass *with clear spirals.*
Right of centre: *The mended bead.*
Left of Centre: *Broken bead.*

(After Baring-Gould et al., 1900.)

Shrines and Burials

The Iron Age Celts were not so much concerned with the After-world as with the Other-world: a region aside from place and time, and unshackled from the conventions of physicality. The Other-world was a place alongside the fort or the field or the feasting-hearth to which some had access at special times, and to and from which others came and went. Certain places and elements were common to both worlds: fires, particular rivers, springs, wooded places, special animals and special nights. The gods were a meddlesome, quarrelsome, interactive lot, much given to shape-changing and rôle-playing, and not above acting as *agents provocateurs* when things got dull. What they had which was divine was integration in the natural world. It seems to have been the Druids' function to interpret and, if possible, manage the philosophy behind this meeting of nature and human experience. Part moral philosophers, part magi, they may (it is not clear) have been at the top of the priestly caste. Different functions were ascribed to the Vates, diviners who deciphered the physical signs of the Other-world, and the Bards, who were praise-singers and, by extension, keepers of the tribal history. The few shrines, statuettes and images which have survived all show the influence of the classical world, which liked its divinities to be regularised and properly depicted so that you knew which god was up to what. There is no indication that the Celts 'worshipped' - only that they 'made contact'. It is likely that most of these meetings of worlds happened in special places - not like the rectangular shrine under the

Heathrow runways, but by springs (like the source of the Seine) or in particular stands of trees. There is a reproduction 'shrine' in the woods below Castell Henllys which, emotionally at least, may come very close to the mark.

Despite the hillforts and the numerous settlements in Preseli, there are no graves - no sign of the Iron Age dead. Certainly the marking of a burial in these times was not a matter of significance, and our modern perception that 'Celtic' deaths (especially in battle) were celebrated in song rather than stone may reflect some part of the truth in the western areas of Britain. There are cist graves in Wales, and burials at the foot of existing standing stones, but nothing in the way of newly erected monuments. Elsewhere in Britain, with a few very notable exceptions, the story is much the same until the century before the Roman Conquest, when a new emphasis on burial with rich and wonderful grave-goods returns in parts of England. Apart from these exceptions, the usual practice is taken to have been the scattering of cremated ashes on water - which, by its very nature, is forever unverifiable.

Just west of Preseli at Castle Bucket, nearly four miles (6km) south of Fishguard, the cremated bones of two adults and a child in one pit and an adult female in an adjoining one were discovered during ploughing. They had been buried beneath a shale slab with a number of cattle bones, and probably a single pig leg-bone disturbed by the plough, just outside the bank of a large defended settlement. A radio-carbon date obtained from the charcoal with the bones gave a late Iron Age date. The bones, however, were oddly selected - too many long bones to too little skull. The Celtic obsession with the head is well-known, and it may be that this burial represents ritual rather than peaceful deaths. There is evidence in Britain for cannibalistic ritual at this time, and it is accepted that this combination of burned human and cattle long bones may be another instance of it.

Northwards, in S. Ceredigion, a pair of 'spoons' was found in the 1850s near, if not in, some form of cairn - the record is unclear. There are several of these pairs of 'spoons' with Iron Age La Tène decoration in Britain and Ireland, often associated with burials, and these definitely suggest some contact with the context which produced the

A pair of ceremonial 'spoons' apparently found in an Iron Age burial mound at Castell Nadolig, S. Ceredigion. (After Barnwell, 1882.) The originals are in the National Museum of Wales, copies in Carmarthen Museum.

1400 BC - AD56

This mirror-handle found near Fishguard is an inartistic example of the finely designed Celtic mirror-handles, and may date to Romano-British times. (After Boon, 1978-80.)

wonderfully rich graves of southern England. The mirror handle from a Fishguard cairn points in the same direction. At the same time, in South Wales, there is some element of a return to the hallowed sites of the Bronze Age. Burials, including several small children, were twice placed close to a standing stone at Stackpole (in Ulster this return to the archaic was so pronounced that a complex of timber-rings almost identical to the Early Bronze Age prototypes was constructed). Preseli would seem to have been open to a variety of different aspects of death-practice, and this must reflect an equal confluence of cultural and perhaps social traits.

Whether the use of Iron Age sites for Early Christian burial is a continuation of this archaism is doubtful.

Romans

When the Second Legion Augustus marched into that part of Britain which was to become Wales, the Celtic world did not plunge into immediate darkness, but every succeeding year the lights dimmed a little more. Three hundred and fifty years later the legions withdrew from Britain, and for a brief while in Wales and the North old sparks flared up. Tales and epics told about and to those generations lie beneath the great Celtic story-cycles which survived - over-laid, twisted, Romanised and Christianised - to be written down in mediaeval times. How much of those strange, shadowy under-stories actually has its origins in the old Celtic world is unknowable, but it is not quite impossible that they are echoes of the tales told to the tale-tellers by the last tale-keepers of prehistory.

Silver trumpet-brooch from Carmarthen.

On this grandiose adornment the regimented regularity of Roman taste has obliterated all the evocative assymmetry of Celtic design. Now in Carmarthenshire Museum.

(Based on Delaney & Wilson, undated.)

GAZETTEER

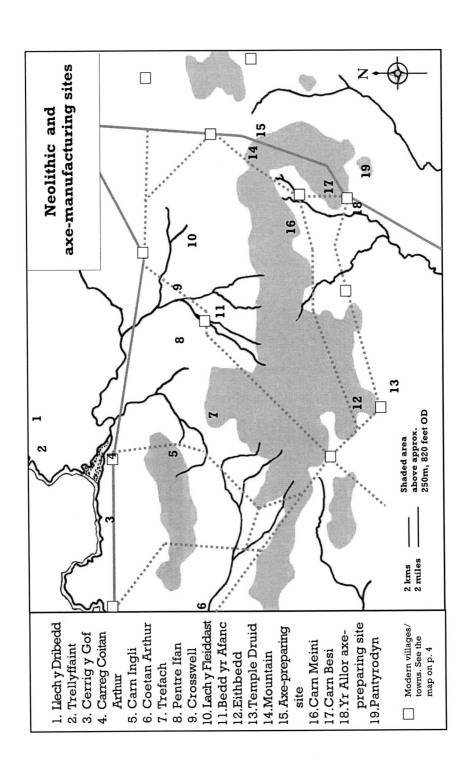

Neolithic and axe-manufacturing sites

1. Llech y Dribedd
2. Trellyffaint
3. Cerrig y Gof
4. Carreg Coitan Arthur
5. Carn Ingli
6. Coetan Arthur
7. Trefach
8. Pentre Ifan
9. Crosswell
10. Lach y Fleiddast
11. Bedd yr Afanc
12. Eithbedd
13. Temple Druid
14. Mountain
15. Axe-preparing site
16. Carn Meini
17. Carn Besi
18. Yr Allor axe-preparing site
19. Pantyrodyn

☐ Modern villages/ towns. See the map on p. 4

Shaded area above approx. 250m, 820 feet OD

2 kms
2 miles

MESOLITHIC SITES

Newport Bridge and sands; SN 0540 & SN 0639: The only Mesolithic site (as opposed to isolated find) in the area (see p. 10). Several groups of microliths and flint debris were found in the drowned land surfaces under the sand, and below the peat on the estuary clays. The public path which runs along the south edge of the estuary from the bridge to the harbour passes, at SN 06163945, the site where the Traeth Mawr flints were found below the peat. There is nothing to see now, but the depth of the peat and the clay below show the situation in which the first discovery was made in 1922. Many of the great variety of water-fowl which live and visit here are the same as those which the Mesolithic flint-knappers were preparing to take.

NEOLITHIC SITES

The two entries at the beginning of this section are rather out of our area, but they have been included because they are well-known and visually very rewarding, and also because they are in a fertile area connected to Preseli by the Nevern river-system.

1. Llech y Dribedd; SN 101432: Now just the heavy-weight chamber of a tomb. Three uprights are still upstanding like an ungainly milking-stool, with a massive 4ft deep capstone still in place and beside it a fallen stone which may be a fourth upright. References have often been made to two stones thrown into the hedge fifty yards to the west. These may have come from the tomb structure, but the field has recently been ploughed and further clearances have made them difficult to distinguish amongst many others. No more than 4ft high inside the chamber, this is a less than graceful structure, but it has great presence. It has been suggested that, as with other tombs in the area, the capstone may never have been covered completely, and that the tomb was never sealed by a closing slab. Since this is so unlike the forbiddingly restricted or concealed entrances to other chambered tomb types, it is possible that a surrounding screen of hurdles or a free-standing wall may have been used, and demolished when the tomb was sealed at the end of its functional life. However, there is no evidence for any such screen. Similar apparently open tombs are found in Northern Ireland. While Llech y Dribedd is usually classified as a Portal Dolmen, some archaeologists suspect that it may have been just a simple, single chamber. The size and shape of any covering mound is unknown - mound traditions are powerful indicators, and critical to fitting remnant chambers into any sort of temporal or

Llech y Dribedd chamber

spatial scheme. There is public access up the lane beside Penlan Farm off the northern-most unnumbered coast road (the lane is used by farm machinery and should not be blocked). The site is over a stile leading from the left-hand fork at the top of the lane - first impressions to be savoured!

2. Trellyffaint; SN 08224252: Probably a true Portal Dolmen with an additional side-chamber, best known for its cup-marked capstone. Remains of the mound are visible here, and it is thought to have been a long one, running north-west/south-east and embracing both chambers. Alternatively, it may have become long by the addition of a second mound abutting on the original and covering the small side-chamber. The chamber itself is defined by the two front portal stones and the smaller back stone. Spaces between these were probably sealed by dry-stone walling and subsidiary uprights like that on the east side. Resting upon these were, probably, two capstones. The hindmost is still there; the front one, which would have rested on top and forward of it, like a lintel above the portal stones, is missing. The existing capstone has split, and what looks like a second stone lying aslant, half in the chamber, is the part which has sheered off. It is on the top of the capstone that the famous cup-marks and the long groove (?'decoration') can be seen. If possible, it is best to visit them in slanting evening light when they are at their most dramatic. While most cup-marked stones seem to have been so insigned in the Early Bronze Age, the practice may have started very much earlier, possibly in Scotland. There, and in Ireland, sloping earthfast boulders are often cup-marked, and the bare capstone of the Trellyffaint chamber may have been treated as if it were one of these. Unlike the best cup-marks, these do not show distinctive boring-rills, and occasional murmurs of scepticism have been heard, but most authorities accept them, at least for the time being.

Cup-marks on the Trellyffaint capstone

The side chamber is a small rectangle defined by three stones set on edge, two on the north-west and one on the south-east. Any cover or closing slab has gone. It opens in a direction slightly different from the main chamber beside it, which is one reason for supposing that it may be a lean-to style addition. No finds or any helpful indicators of date have ever been recovered.

Permission to visit the tomb, which is in private fields, must be asked from Trellyffaint Farm, who will provide directions appropriate to current field-use. The tomb cannot be seen from any road or lane.

There is a standing stone (**66**) to the south-east (no access), directly beyond the putative line of the suggested long mound; whether it is an outlier or a coincidence is debatable. It can be seen as a hump-backed rather wide stone low down near the marshy area of the same field.

Another cup-marked stone stands near a hedgerow a couple of miles due south, just across the present B4582 road at **Trefael (SN 103403)**. The position of this triangular tilted stone can be seen from a public footpath which crosses the field where it stands, but unfortuntely does not go right up to it. It is not known whether this is the capstone of a demolished tomb or a decorated earth-fast slab.

Tredissi, SN 074419, SE of Llech y Dribedd, may be the site of yet another chambered tomb. If so, this would indicate an impressive line of monuments running south-west/north-east above the Nyfer river-system and vaguely opposite Pentre Ifan and Bedd yr Afanc on the Preseli side.

3. Cerrig y Gof; SN 03653890: This is a very peculiar monument. In essence it is an oval mound with five small rectangular chambers set in it, all facing outwards like the spokes of a wheel. There are a few other chambered tombs of vaguely similar pattern in western Scotland and eastern Ireland, but they are rare and none is really very similar. Fenton, the early nineteenth-century Pembrokeshire antiquarian, explored it when it was already in much the same state as it is today, and found some black pebbles (unusual - white quartz is common), charcoal and bits of unburned human bone along with what he described as sherds of the 'rudest' pottery, all now sadly lost. The adjective suggests that the pottery was late, as earlier Neolithic tomb wares tend to be better made, and the small separate 'box' tombs at Cerrig y Goff are in many ways as akin to Early Bronze Age cists as they are to Neolithic chambers. There is no real indication of date, however. The tomb has been seen as an idiosyncratic answer to a specific need - perhaps the untoward collective deaths of a caste or dynasty through plague or battle. None of the chambers has a closing stone, which is stretching co-incidence, as the only missing roof-slab (which would be the first to be dismantled deliberately) is known to have been used for a bridge; presumably they were never sealed (cf. **1**). The largest chamber would seem to be the northern-most, at the point of the oval mound, and the most elaborate now is the south-eastern chamber, where additional stones at the entrance give it the appearance of a mini Portal Dolmen.

A large monolith at the west side of the same field is pitted in a way that suggests cup-marks; another, nearer the road hedge, may be a further associated fallen stone. Together with the five chambers, this would make an impressive arrangement with superficial resemblances to some of the features at both Llech y Dribedd (**1**) and Trellyffaint (**2**). The landowner

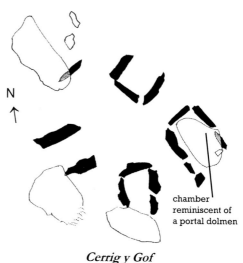

chamber
reminiscent of
a portal dolmen

N
↑

Cerrig y Gof

The entrances to the five chambers are so positioned that they could only be entered from a banana-shaped or irregular mound. It is just possible that one or more may have been sealed cists rather than chambers.
(Simplified from Lynch, 1972.)

generously allows visitors into the field, which is in constant use. Access is through the field gate on the Dinas side of the steep little dip in the main road at Holmus Farm, with parking in the lay-by above on the Newport side.

69

4. Carreg Coitan Arthur; SN 06023935: A well-known and much photographed tomb. Recent hedge-cutting has restored the relationship of this marvellous monument with its surroundings, especially its rare proximity to the estuary which can now be seen behind it. An enormous ridge-backed capstone is supported on only two small protruberances of the four stones of the chamber. It is usually described unequivocally as a Portal Dolmen, but recent excavations have revealed peculiarities of the mound and the structure of the chamber, which used not to be apparent. Details of these findings were unpublished at the time of writing. It was assumed that the 'front' of the tomb had the classic H-structure of the Portal Dolmen, and that the gap on the south-east was the result of the second upright of the H having fallen and been removed. The excavation appears to show that no such stone had ever been there; no third stone, no portal. An arc of small stones had been laid like a kerb around at least the southern side of the remains of the mound, and between it and the chamber the ground had been cleared of stones. Right in front of the chamber (if it is now a 'front') there had been a platform under which some broken pottery and clumps of cremated human bone had been sealed; and away from the platform, but also outside the chamber, more cremation material and a slightly different sort of pottery were found (both within a western 'Abingdon' tradition), looking as if each deposit had been laid in a specially designated area. Radio-carbon dating puts the construction of the chamber as early as 3500 BC, that is, the middle of the Neolithic period. In what was left of the prehistoric fill inside the chamber some sherds of Grooved Ware and Beaker Ware were found, indicating that the interior had been disturbed, if not used, at a much later date. This excavation has called into question both how our chambered tombs can - or even whether they should - be labelled, and how we should view their prolonged and changing functions.

Signposted on the road out of the east end of Newport, which leads *via* the bridge to the beach and golf course, the site is in a small enclosure a hundred yards into the housing-estate. Parking on the side road only.

Carreg Coitan Arthur

The capstone, closing-stone and left-hand upright look like components of a classic Portal Dolmen, but the gap on the right side of the closing stone now seems to be an original feature.

Carreg Coitan Arthur is one of the only sites in Preseli where there is any evidence for the use of the fascinating Beaker pottery.

5. Carn Ingli; SN 063376: There are rectangular and circular huts in the hillfort (see pp. 25-6) which, it has been suggested, might date from the late Neolithic, but it is extremely difficult to pick these out among the havoc of strewn boulders among the crags. Similar hill-tops at Clegyr Boia near St. David's and Carn Brea in Cornwall, amongst others, were fortified and defensively employed at this time. It is tempting to imagine that some fateful event on Carn Ingli might be the reason for the curious chambers at Cerrig y Gof!

6. Coetan Arthur; SN 007361: Site of a chambered tomb which wreaked revenge on the farmer who demolished it in 1844 to build himself a new house in which he endured nothing but ill luck. At Tre-llwyn Fawr, also above Cwm Gwaun at SN 002355, an apparent standing stone may be the remains of another of which the capstone was seen in the mid-nineteenth century. There is no access. These two possible tombs belong more properly to the Fishguard series than to the Preseli area.

7. Trefach; SN 06393505: This may have been the site of a chambered tomb, of which a standing stone (**73**) may be the only remaining upright. The large stone lying in the field to its left has been suggested as a possible capstone. It is in a plausible position for a Neolithic tomb. There is no access, but from the unnumbered road running south from Cilgwyn both stones can be seen in a field east of the road and south of Trefach farm.

8. Pentre Ifan; SN 09943701: The most famous of all the Preseli sites, and one of the most beautiful prehistoric silhouettes in Britain; well worth seeing twice, once at dusk. The tomb is poised on a wide, gently sloping terrace above the Nyfer river valley and facing the crags of Carnedd Meibion Owen. Its extraordinary combination of massively wide but kindly proportioned capstone, minimally supported on pointed orthostats and fronted by a magnificent facade curved in two dimensions, is so light and lofty that it is hard to believe either that it was not meant to be seen in its entirety, or that it is just a happy accident. However, it is so rare for a megalithic monument to coincide with our modern perception of 'beauty', that a unique accident is probably what it is.

An information board is provided on site, and the details given here are intended to supplement, not duplicate, its contents. Pentre Ifan is the one 'classic' Portal Dolmen in Preseli, having the H-shaped unmovable frontage and stone-lined chamber directly behind. The closing slab is set well back from the matched flanking uprights, both of which have a sinuous concave profile which enhances the forbidding quality of the flat expanse of the central stone - that much at least may not be unintentional. The floor of the chamber may have been formed by the pit left when the capstone was lifted up on to its supporters - implying that it was already there and the site selected to incorporate it. Today the chamber has no side stones, but the stone-holes which held the two on the west side were found during excavation, and one of the stones still lies where it fell, outwards, to the side of the chamber. There were no matching stone-holes on the east side, which must therefore have had non-weight-bearing 'propped' stones or drystone walling, as was found elsewhere, filling gaps between large stones. Alternatively it may have been open altogether, as at Carreg Coitan Arthur (**4**). The large monolith in the grass behind the facade on the east (right side, facing the front) was found to have been an upright stone which had been laid flat before the mound was built over it. The fallen and broken stones in front are the remains of the facade, which extended out further on each side than it does now. This facade created a sort of

NEOLITHIC SITES:
4400-2400 BC

'forecourt' which was filled in, sealing the tomb, at the end of its functional life.

There are three current interpretations of Pentre Ifan. It was excavated in the late 1930s and again by the same archaeologist, W.F. Grimes, twenty years later. He took the tomb to be an entity, a Portal Dolmen elaborated by a fine facade and an unusually long mound, which had been built over a downthrown stone and some fire pits. Later, in the light of discoveries elsewhere, another archaeologist, Frances Lynch, re-interpreted Grimes' findings and suggested that the original structure had been the H-shaped Portal Dolmen backed by a small, squarish mound over or around the chamber, and that this whole edifice had been enlarged and elaborated by the subsequent addition of the long mound and augmented facade. Most recently, and again in the light of yet more discoveries, a third theory has been put forward, suggesting that the single stone (then upstanding) and the firepits were one element of a dual mortuary site, of which the Portal Dolmen was the second structure, and that these two together were covered by the long mound when the site (for whatever reason) ceased to be ritually functional.

The information board provided on site gives only Grimes' interpretation. The outlines given above are mere sketches of the sequences envisaged by subsequent re-analysis, without any of the detailed reasoning which lies behind them, but the mere fact that the tomb can be interpreted in such different ways serves to point up how little is really known about what actually happened, even in the face of expert excavation, and how the information gained by new discoveries changes the

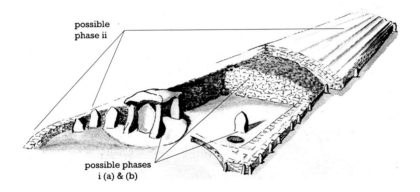

Possible interpretation of the evolution of Pentre Ifan chambered tomb.

i(a): *The standing stone and one of the fire-pits are shown as they must have been before any mound was raised.*

i(b): *The actual chamber with the short mound (or enclosure) and simple, unembellished façade may then have existed as a complete chambered tomb either engulfing the felled stone, or as part of a complex with it.*

ii: *The elongated tapering mound and the elaborated façade covered the whole of the earlier structure.*

The only direct structural evidence for this multi-phase interpretation is the line of small retaining uprights shown here on the right side of the inner mound, and the existence of the felled standing stone. The final act was the sealing of the portal and forecourt with carefully laid slabs (not shown).

(Following Lynch, 1972, and Barker, 1992.)

focus of established facts. This is a continual process in archaeology, and often leads to the impression that an earlier interpretation is 'wrong'; however, all interpretations are no more than ideas based on the accumulated evidence available at the time (with varying degrees of insight and flair thrown in).

Nothing found in the excavation favours any of the three projected sequences. The objects retrieved were few: a flint scraper of a type common in Ireland was found on the old ground surface under the mound, a broken triangular arrowhead on the edge of the chamber-pit in front of the eastern portal stone, and white quartz pebbles in the chamber; a flint knife-blade was incorporated in the tomb blocking. Most interesting were pieces of pottery which had been preserved with some gorse charcoal, and a few flint pieces in a sheltered patch of the original chamber, just behind the transverse closing-slab. These were from a particular type of vessel (a carinated bowl) of which they are the only pieces so far found in south-west Wales. It is now thought that these special bowls may have had strictly ritual, even mortuary functions - containers for bits of ancestor rather than dinner. They appear in mortuary contexts in Britain from before 4000 BC onwards, especially in places where chambered tombs were subsequently built. The small pieces of one of these bowls here at Pentre Ifan may refer to rituals of a death which occurred before the 'hallowed' area was encased in the mound, and perhaps not even at Pentre Ifan. The gorse charcoal which was intermingled with these sherds has been taken to indicate that the area around had already been thoroughly cleared, and that the fierce fire of gorse was used as an alternative to less easily available oak. Crushed gorse, however, makes very good fodder, and the charcoal may equally represent a valued resource husbanded in the immediate area.

Signposted as 'Burial Chamber', the site lies among side roads south of the A487 between Newport and Felindre Farchog, or can be reached by sticking tenaciously to one of the small roads going north through Brynberian village (leaving the school on the left). This way the magnificent site and the stone ridge (see below) can be seen to their best advantage. There is parking at the site entrance, and the enclosed area is manageable for wheel-chairs. After visiting, continue seawards down this road for magnificent views of the coast and the position of many prehistoric sites in the landscape.

Stone ridge; SN 099369: A bristling line of upright stones; not a stone row, as once thought, but the result of naturally vertical strata. The western-most stone, however, is tapered and slightly separate, and it just may be a standing stone. This ridge may be the source of the vertical uprights at Pentre Ifan, which directly faces it. There is a startling view of the ridge from a cottage along the Brynberian-Pentre Ifan road, but no access. The ridge can also be seen from the other direction, though less dramatically, from the forecourt of the tomb.

9. Crosswell; SN 120365: An 18th century description indicates that there may have been a burial chamber somewhere here. There are no visible remains.

10. Lach y Fleiddast; SN 1535: Another erstwhile site, possibly of a chambered tomb. No extant remains.

11. Bedd yr Afanc; SN 10883457: The Grave of the Water Monster - definitely not to be approached in wet weather. Known as the only gallery-grave in Wales, this long, narrow tomb now sits on a small 'island' at the lower (north) margin of Brynberian bog. All that is visible are the two long lines of small uprights which form the sides of the gallery (or passage), and the stony dry ground surrounding it. It was excavated in the late 1930s, when it was thought to be a passage-grave, but revealed itself to be more akin to an Irish or Scottish gallery grave, although

NEOLITHIC SITES: 4400-2400 BC

Bedd yr Afanc, looking west into the gallery from the entrance.

without the sills or jambs which divide this sort of tomb into segments or stalls up its length. The mound which once covered it was found to be a stumpy rectangle, possibly defined by a row of smallish stones which were found outside both sides of the tomb. The gallery itself is composed of upright stones set in pairs opposite each other, with a confused area at the inner (west) end which could be interpreted as the remains of a slightly higher, expanded chamber. Bedd yr Afanc is peculiar, whether seen as an Irish wedge tomb, a Scottish gallery grave or an undifferentiated passage grave, fulfilling but few of the criteria of any of these types (some do not even accept it as a chambered tomb at all). An attempt was made in the mid-1980s to date the tomb by botanical methods since the excavation had produced no finds of any sort, but the results did not help to date its construction. It is definitely worth visiting and pondering over, but dry weather is desirable.

There is parking space at the bridge at Brynberian. Walk north-west up the road for about 500 yards and turn right into the bridleway. Follow this past the smallholdings until it opens on to the bog. Turn right and, keeping the fence immediately on the right, follow it round two dog-legs until it obviously turns north back towards the road. From this corner walk south-west for about 200 yards into the bog, and the stones will appear unmistakably amongst the gorse bushes. Not as bad as it sounds, but can be very soggy.

12. Eithbedd; c.SN 079286: A collection of enormous stones piled at the bottom of the third and fourth fields east along the Mynachlog-ddu side road from its junction with the New Inn/Maenclochog road. This is all that is left of two, or possibly three, monuments which seem to have been chambered tombs. There is a plethora of remains in these fields, including a possible ring-cairn and a possible henge (**99**), but they are all in a ruinous condition and cannot really be appreciated from the road. Nonetheless they do form a nucleus of Neolithic sites and possible sites, and it is interesting to see where they are in relation to the lowland on which they abut.

13. Temple Druid; SN 096272: Another interesting possible nucleus, just outside our area but intriguingly close to Eithbedd. A rectangular cropmark, which is undatable, has been seen from the air. Not far from it there are at least three possible chambered tombs and several standing stones. It is marginally within the bounds of possibility, given the vicinity of the other monuments, that the cropmark might be a 'hengiform' structure of an unusual type. There is nothing visible except for one standing stone at SN 09572702, in the field below Prysg Farm.

14. Mountain; SN 16573286: Remains of a collapsed chambered tomb. The size of the stones indicates that it has been a large one, but their relationships to each other and to the capstone are so distorted that it is no longer possible to tell what sort of tomb it was. It was described as having a round mound, the remains of which are still visible, and the length of the fallen stones has suggested that they are 'appropriate' to a Portal Dolmen. Such ruination is sad because the tomb was in an interesting place at the very beginning of the youngest of the Cleddau rivulets, and on the side of a saddle passing between Crug yr Hwch and Foel Drygarn.

The capstone and a fallen supporter can be seen at the bottom of the field opposite the Blaen Llethyr Cattery, a short way south of the beginning of the prehistoric ridgeway track across the hill-tops. The remainder are the other side of the hedge. Permission to visit should be sought at Ietwen Farm.

15. Axe-preparing site; c. SN 185308: There is no access and nothing visible in the spread of fields below Pentre Galar hamlet. Nonetheless, it is fascinating to see the area in which such a major phenomenon in Neolithic life actually, physically, took place (see p. 19).

16. Carn Meini chambered tomb; SN 14043262: A stone cairn which appears to have a chamber within. Most of the capstone is visible, and three of the supporting stones can dimly be seen within (climbing around it is risky as many of the stones are far from steady - on no account attempt to enter). It all seems far too big to qualify as a cist, although the cairn is similar to the Early Bronze Age cairns around. In the collapsed material in front of the chamber a single stone can be seen, apparently earthfast and upstanding. Whether this may be part of a passage is not yet known. Standing on open ground at the head of the 'stone river' on the west end of Carn Meini crags, this may be one of a small group of West Wales tombs which are peculiarly placed under or against such crags. Well worth visiting, it is right beside Carn Meini itself, and can be reached from the ridgeway past Foel Drygarn or by walking up from the unfenced road below Carn Sian and thence east around the back of the cwm.

Carn Meini chambered tomb

The derelict cairn and collapsing capstone of a possible passage grave. The upright stone in the left foreground could be part of a passage.

NEOLITHIC SITES: 4400-2400 BC

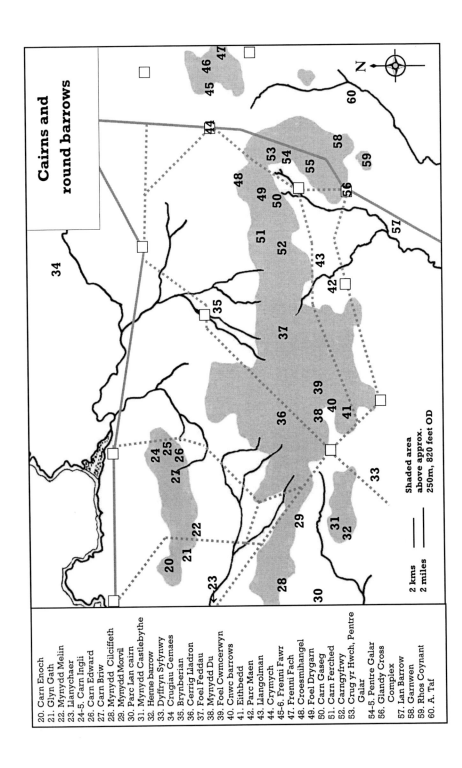

Cairns and round barrows

20. Carn Enoch
21. Glyn Gath
22. Mynydd Melin
23. Llanychaer
24-5. Carn Ingli
26. Carn Edward
27. Carn Briw
28. Mynydd Cilciffeth
29. Mynydd Morvil
30. Parc Lan cairn
31. Mynydd Castlebythe
32. Henne barrow
33. Dyfryn Syfynwy
34. Crugiau Cemaes
35. Brynberian
36. Cerrig Lladron
37. Foel Feddau
38. Mynydd Du
39. Foel Cwmcerwyn
40. Chwc barrows
41. Eithbedd
42. Parc Maen
43. Llangolman
44. Crymych
45-6. Frenni Fawr
47. Frenni Fach
48. Croesmihangel
49. Foel Drygarn
50. Carn Gaseg
51. Carn Ferched
52. Carngyfrwy
53. Crug yr Hwch, Pentre Galar
54-5. Pentre Galar
56. Glandy Cross Complex
57. Lan Barrow
58. Garnwen
59. Rhos Coynant
60. A. Taf

Shaded area
above approx.
250m, 820 feet OD

2 kms
2 miles

N

17. Carn Besi; SN 15632768: A large capstone lies among a group of dispersed stones suggesting a low, or even earthfast chamber, of which there are several in Pembrokeshire. The capstone rests upon supporters at the front, but on the ground at the back. In some cases the chamber is sub-megalithic - dug into the ground so that it is below the surrounding ground level. It is thought that this may be quite an early phenomenon, but in some instances the supporting stones have collapsed inwards under the capstone and thus been rendered invisible. Whether or not this has happened at Carn Besi is not known. There seems little doubt that it is some form of chambered tomb, and as such would be one of the earliest monuments in the vicinity of Glandy Cross. There is no access, but the stones are just over the road-bank opposite the reservoir. Care should be exercised if perching up here - this road carries some very heavy traffic.

18. Yr Allor axe preparing site; SN 138265: Again nothing visible, but the axe-sharpening flakes were found near the standing stones which can be seen from the west of Meini Gwyr. The presence of both these axe-manufacturing sites may have eventually given rise to the extraordinary concentration of ritual sites at Glandy Cross (**56**).

19. Pantyrodyn; SN 15022550: Two upright stones here have been recorded as possibly the remains of a chambered tomb. Equally, they may be two standing stones (cf. **104**).

BRONZE AGE CAIRNS, BARROWS AND BURIAL SITES

There are nearly sixty of these funerary monuments in Preseli, but the majority of them are now indistinct and a great number are in enclosed fields without access. Only those about which some detail is known, which are in some way spectacular or which are easily accessible are featured in this gazetteer.

20. Carn Enoch; SN 01263705: A lovely site, very clear on the ground as a raised ring of earth and stone just under the north-east of the crag, with wonderful views. (See the photograph on page 78.) There are easily found footpaths to the crags from the T junction to the south-east. Ring-cairn burial monuments and later Iron Age hut foundations are not always easily distinguishable, and this circle is not in a place actually typical of either!

21. Glyn Gath; SN 01673662: Another ring-cairn/Iron Age hut foundation on a low plateau below Carn Enoch (**20**). The stone and earth bank is very clearly defined.

22. Mynydd Melyn; SN 02853638: Not very distinct cairn or barrow base. The small stone just to the north-west may be a standing stone associated with it. Beside the footpath from Glyn Gath (above) to Bedd Morris to the east, just east of where the major tracks cross very close to **112**.

23. Llanychaer; SM 97543537: This cairn is now destroyed. It seems to have been a hillside cairn, possibly with a sort of passage leading to a cist, within which an

BRONZE AGE SITES:
2500-1400 BC

Carn Enoch: Probably a ring-carn, it is also occasionally cited as a good example of an Iron Age hut-circle.

Carn Edward: Sometimes described as possible ring-cairns, the three circular banks are most likely to be the foundations of Iron Age huts.

Early Bronze Age urn, now in the National Museum of Wales, was found with burnt bone and quartz.

24. Carn Ingli; SN 063378: Round barrow or barrows in the area below and to the north of the hillfort, amongst hut foundations and a standing stone. The barrow is not universally accepted, but it is hard to distinguish which is what down here!

25. Carn Ingli; SN 05323668: A supposed kerb cairn (a cairn with a setting of large stones around the perimeter - see p. 34). It is not universally accepted, and is hard to distinguish amongst the boulders and huts on the summit.

BRONZE AGE SITES:
2500-1400 BC

78

26. Carn Edward; SN 05493681: Three readily visible distinct raised circles on the slope of the hill, two thirds of the way downhill between Carn Briw (**27**) and the natural crags of Carn Edward. The burial v. hut uncertainty applies here, too. This site is well worth seeing, as it is so well-defined and also has glorious views.

27. Carn Briw; SN 05633706: One of the grand hill-top cairns. Made of smallish stones, Carn Briw still stands up to 8ft high. It has been subject to some rootling in modern times and has a recently constructed mini-cairn on the side, which spoils its profile. Visible from considerable distances.

28. Mynydd Cilciffeth; SN 009324: The hill-top cairns up here have been destroyed. The area is undergoing improvement, and the enormous mounds on the summit, which look like cairns, are actually clearance mounds (probably accidentally replicating the Bronze Age appearance).

29. Mynydd Morvil; SN 039313: Aerial photography has recently shown up what may be a barrow-cemetery here. Not appreciable on the ground.

30. Parc Lan cairn; SN 006309: A small low-lying stony cairn, just visible from the roadside, in rough pasture. An interesting contrast to the high cairns overlooking it from Mynydd Castlebythe.

31. Mynydd Castlebythe; SN 028296: Two huge hill-top cairns, very close together. The one with the trig. point atop is otherwise undisturbed, but the second was investigated at the beginning of the century and found to contain 'nothing but charcoal', so may have been used for a cremation burial at some point. Approach by the path which runs round the back of the mountain from the unfenced road. Direct ascent by instinct is not recommended!

32. Henne barrow, Castlebythe; SN 02062723: A small round barrow, significant because it lies above and on the periphery of the Wallis Moor area, which may have been enclosed in Bronze Age times (see p. 46), and may therefore be the burial place of a direct progenitor of those early stockmen. No obvious viewing point.

33. Dyffryn Syfynwy ring-cairn; SN 05922845: Also known as Dyffryn henge and Dyffryn circle. (See the picture on p. 35.) This burial site feels quite different from the gaunt cairns on the hill-tops. Although the centre is still a stone mound, it is tightly enclosed by a ring of ten upstanding and two fallen uprights. The cairn is now only about 1m high, so the uprights may look more like a circle than they did when the cairn was fresh. It certainly appears much more like a stone circle than the ringed platform above Meini Gwyr (see p. 91). One stone, on the east side of the mound, is taller and more pointed than its peers, and may have been significant. Despite seeming overgrown and abandoned, the site retains a somewhat forbidding air, and is well worth seeing as a most unusual monument. Access is by the public footpath two fields west of the reservoir (very muddy in wet weather!), and the same path gives splendid views of the position of the Budloy Stone (**85**), which it subsequently passes, across the A. Syfynwy. Whether there is any relationship between these two fine monuments facing each other across the river is unknown.

34. Crugiau Cemaes barrow cemetery; SN 12504154: Rather outside the area, but a splendid and easily reached example of a cemetery of large barrows. These four stand on a low hill, locally very prominent but not a landmark for miles like the big hill-top cairns. There is public access by a short path, and parking space. The barrows

BRONZE AGE SITES:
2500-1400 BC

Crugiau Cemaes barrow-cemetery from the west.

were first recorded in our era in 1695, but when they were explored in the last century a coin dated to AD 69 was turned up. The Romans were very superstitious about ancient burial places, and often left a nervous gratuity when they disturbed them. As well as the coin, five urns with bones and ashes were recovered (one is in the Ashmolean Museum in Oxford).

35. Brynberian; SN 112351: A scatter of the sort of white quartz which is such a feature of Neolithic and Bronze Age sites has led to the recording of a possible barrow here. There is no other sign above ground.

36. Cerrig Lladron hill-top cairn; SN 06583208: A magnificent hill-top cairn, still nearly 7ft high and with a massive circumference, somewhat dented in places. Unusually, this one stands alone. The line of summits crowned by cairns, which runs east along the rideway, is a remarkable sight. The individual position each group occupies on the range is clearly perceptible, while at the same time the whole of the top of the Preselis looks like one extended linear cemetery. For an appreciation of the landscape of Preseli and the detail of the topography below, this is an unbeatable viewpoint. It is hard not to wonder who won the right to lie alone in such an incomparable place.

Cerrig Lladron hill-top cairn

BRONZE AGE SITES:
2500-1400 BC

37. Foel Feddau hill-top cairn; SN 10223236: Another large, single cairn beside the ridgeway. Recorded as 200ft in diameter, it is stone built, but turf has grown over it.

38. Mynydd Du cairn; SN 07953119: This small cairn, very damaged, is one of a series running round the breast of the mountain, well below the hill-top cairns.

39. Foel Cwmcerwyn hill-top cairns; SN 094312: A fine group of four large cairns, the highest still standing up to 5ft. Follow the forestry fence on the outside of the wire where it leaves the ridgeway track and runs uphill and almost due south. After a very short distance the grass-covered cairns show up on the skyline. In 1806 the western cairn, which is quite large, was excavated by Fenton, who found a cremation in an upside-down urn. Just east of it is the second cairn, which he also opened but where he found nothing. Beyond them are two more, the smaller of which also appeared empty. The larger of these seems to have a flat top like some of the barrows at Glandy Cross (**56**). The depressions made by the excavations are very obvious.

Urn burial

40. Cnwc barrows; SN 08563027: This round barrow has been described as a type known as a 'bell'-barrow (see **46**), as it has a distinct central mound. It has been suggested that this mound is perhaps a ruined lime kiln, though it may have been set on an original barrow. The second barrow, at SN 08763046, is undisputed, and one of the few in this rocky area which shows traces of a surrounding ditch on the S side. At the time of writing these barrows were both inaccessible. Forestry harvesting will change this eventually.

41. Eithbedd; SN 08152920: Yet another site in this crowded area. This one, possibly a ring-barrow, is in enclosed land and out of sight over the convex shoulder of the hill. At SN 07972864 there is another possible ring-barrow down on the other side of the road, near the hedge on the east side of the B4313. It is occasionally visible from above as an indistinct smudge in the grass.

42. Parc Maen; SN 11342833: Recent excavations of what appeared to be a barrow with outlying stones have unravelled the long history of this complex site. The sequence of events here is described and illustrated on pages 39 and 82. The site, which is on a wide, gently sloping shelf above the Cleddau, is on enclosed land and there is no direct access to it. Perhaps the most intriguing aspect of Parc Maen is the series of additions and re-uses to which the site was put, each phase either incorporating or scrupulously avoiding previous structures. The same site seems to have held its importance for nearly a thousand years - a remarkable instance of fidelity to a special place.

43. Llangolman; SN 1228: An urn containing 'bones and things' was found not far from the right bank of the river. It could have come from a previously levelled barrow, or might just have been an urn burial from much later in the Bronze Age, when barrows were no longer built.

BRONZE AGE SITES:
2500-1400 BC

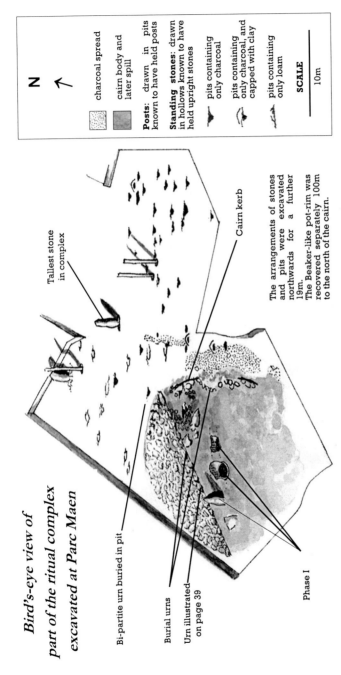

Bird's-eye view of part of the ritual complex excavated at Parc Maen

N ↑

charcoal spread

cairn body and later spill

Posts: drawn in pits known to have held posts

Standing stones: drawn in hollows known to have held upright stones

pits containing only charcoal

pits containing only charcoal, and capped with clay

pits containing only loam

SCALE

10m

Tallest stone in complex

Bi-partite urn buried in pit

Burial urns

Urn illustrated on page 39

Cairn kerb

Phase I

The arrangements of stones and pits were excavated northwards for a further 19m.
The Beaker-like pot-rim was recovered separately 100m to the north of the cairn.

Phase 1: Burial site? The larger of the two pits under the cairn may have held a crouched burial which has not survived; the smaller was a fire-pit. The low standing stone beside them was erected before the cairn, perhaps at the same time as the burial.
Phase 2: Ritual site. The cairn was raised, several inurned deposits were incorporated in it, and beside it a number of pits were opened, some to be filled purely with charcoal, others purely with loam, and a few with a mixture of the two. A number of smallish standing stones and a few posts were erected, and a spread of charcoal stained the ground outside the cairn edge. An urn was buried upside-down among them.
Phase 3: Generations later, another urn of a much later type was put into the now ancient cairn.

(Based on Marshall, 1991.)

44. Crymych; SN 18133377: Situated on the edge of the marshy ground to the north-west, and on the line of the ridgeway between Foel Drygarn and the Frenni Fawr, this may well have been a wayside barrow. If so, it may have been linked either to Croesmihangel and the barrows below Foel Drygarn, or to the barrows on Pentre Galar. The site is protected and therefore preserved, but visually it is now immersed in the gardens of the first houses on the north side of the Llain Drigarn estate, opposite the Fire Station.

45. Frenni Fawr foot; SN 198341: This erstwhile barrow is now only an imperceptible irregularity.

46. Frenni Fawr hill-top barrows; SN 2035: There are five barrows on this separate outlier of the Preselis, three together at the top and one lower down on either side. Coming up from the Castellan side, just south of Blaenffos (this narrow road is used by farm machinery, so it is best to park back by the bungalows), a stiled track leads up on to the mountain. The first barrow is below the summit on the right of the path at SN 19943517. This was opened by Fenton, and in either this or in the bell-barrow opposite it on the other side of the hill-top - the record is not clear - he found the remains of a cremation in an urn in a stone cist. This was well below signs of another, later burial which had been put into the barrow above it. Whichever of these two barrows it was that he explored was used again after the original deposition of the urn in the cist. On the summit of the hill, at SN 203350, he found that the first barrow had already been dug into, and he recovered nothing. The adjacent barrow (of the type known as 'bowl-barrow' - see p. 34), is also deeply excavated. The third of this group, now the largest of all, is crowned by a trig. stone. At nearly 6ft high even today, this must have been a magnificent monument. Further along the eastern path down from the summit the fifth barrow, at SN 20643474, is the other contender for Fenton's urn cremation. The last of this quintet is lower down, on a small 'shelf' in the grass field, just where the fence turns away to the left and the footpath (unfortunately for the barrow) actually goes across it. This side barrow is of a type called 'bell'-barrows, which is supposed to suggest the round mound with a space (berm) between it and the surrounding ditch. Bell-barrows are rare in Preseli, and it is strange that there is one up here on this isolated hill. In Wessex, where bell-barrows are one among several different round-barrow styles which are scattered over the chalk in their hundreds, they usually cover male burials, and are thought to be generally a little later than the plainer bowl barrow. In purely visual terms, it could appear that the prime position on the Frenni Fawr had already been occupied, but that there was something about this particular hill, set apart from the rest, which made it appropriate for the rare bell-barrow. The surrounding ditch of a bell-barrow may not have been just a way of gathering up material for the mound;

Frenni Fawr - skyline barrow hollowed by old excavation.

BRONZE AGE SITES:
2500-1400 BC

indeed the styling of round barrows - some with no berm at all, others (disc barrows) with an inconveniently wide one - suggests that the ditch had a space-defining function of its own, perhaps serving the same sort of purpose as the quartz pavements and large boulders which surround burial places in this more stony part of Britain. The Frenni barrows lead one to wonder whether they cover strangers, not prepared to bury their dead amongst the resident poulation.

47. Frenni Fach hill-top barrow; SN 22593486: Quite distinct, this may have been a large barrow, but it has been dug into and seriously damaged. Access is by paths from the track along the side of the hill. This is the eastern end of the long line of hill-top cairns.

48. Croesmihangel round barrow; SN 16453323: Only the remains, full of pits, hollows, dumps and sheep-scrapes, are now visible. Two opposite quadrants of the barrow were excavated in the late 1950s after a sheep had kindly dug an urn out of her sheltering spot, and another four urns were recovered. These were of a type known as tripartite urns and, unusually, these had decoration on their deep collars. They can be seen in Tenby Museum, where the two cremations found have been carefully and decently replaced in the urns in which they were originally buried. Four of the five urns had been placed in stone-lined cists under a clayey platform, two upside down on their own and two, of which one stood on its base, side by side in a mutual cist. The platform itself lay on top of a deep layer of charcoal, and also covered a pit which had been filled with more charcoal. It had been surrounded by an uneven ditch, and the upcast used in the platform. A row of ten stakes had been driven into the platform, very close together - possibly the uprights of light hurdlng. Other post holes near the perimeter may represent a post circle. In effect this created a flat but architecturally structured urn cemetery. Not much later the structure made by the hurdling-stakes was removed, and a barrow raised over the platform. This was made of turves and earth with bits of burnt stone and charcoal mixed in it, and a retaining kerb of quartz around it. The fifth urn was dug right through the bottom layers of the mound, and had obviously been put in a short while after the original four. It was considered too small to hold a complete cremation, so it may have contained a small amount of a cremation moved from elsewhere. The urns are of a type which were current late on in the Early Bronze Age, perhaps as much as five hundred years after the construction of Meini Gwyr, and later than the great hill-top cairns on Foel Drygarn.

49. Foel Drygarn; SN 15753358: Of these three enormous stone cairns only one has been subjected to early exploration, but nothing was found. Their size can only be appreciated by standing among them; one is still nearly 3m high. Two are set so close that the spill from each is actually touching; the third has but a modicum of clear space. They are visible for decades of miles around, more so than any of the other hill-top cairns, and as this must have been as apparent in the Bronze Age as it is now, they may have been the first or the principal cairns on the ridgeway.

The prehistoric ridgeway track: Many paths lead up to Foel Drygarn at the beginning of the track which appears to follow the prehistoric way from the Frennis to Mynydd Cilciffeth or Carn Ingli. The stretch westwards from Croesmihangel to the road (B 4329) under Foel Eryr, is particularly spectacular, taking in a number of Bronze and Iron Age sites, and giving bird's-eye views of the topographical placing of many more. On a fair day there are views of the ancient land and sea routes from Ireland to Milford Haven, and the significance of the siting of the great cairns up here all along this astonishing route is inescapable. A map and a pair of stout boots (parts of the mountain are boggy/muddy at all times of the year) can deliver an awesome experience. It can be very cold up here, and the weather changes extremely quickly. There are quite enough paths through the heather or round the wet parts to reach all the sites, and they should be kept to - there are seriously deep patches of dangerous bog. The ideal way to cover the ridgeway is on horseback, and there are stables at either end (under no circumstances should anyone ever attempt to take a horse off the main track without a local guide, no

Foel Drygarn, from Croesmihangel, showing the ramparts and three hill-top cairns. The ridgeway strikes off to the left.

matter how dry and solid the track itself may seem). Enclosed public theme parks are often described as a 'walk through history'; a few tramps between Croesmihangel and Cerrig Lladron are far more than that - they are an experience of prehistory.

50. Carn Gaseg; SN 15973303: A ring cairn, not easy to find in the heather, just on the north side of the track half way between Croesmihangel and the forestry fence.

51. Carn Ferched; SN 15273299: A circular cairn. Turn north into the heather about fifty yards west of the giant boulder on the outside of the forestry fence. The cairn is on the moor, another fifty yards or so straight on through the heather. It makes an interesting contrast with the great cairns above on Foel Drygarn.

52. Carngyfrwy; SN 14453260: A round barrow - really hard to find, but it *is* there among the rock protrusions and lumps just to the north of the track downhill from the north-west of Carn Meini. The two stone-heaps at SN 14113299 are likely to be cairns, too. The upstanding stone in one of them indicates that these are probably more than clearance cairns. These may form a discreet little wayside cemetry of different (or lesser?) stature than the magnificent hill-top cairns on either side of them. These definitely look over the north side of the hills.

53. Crug yr Hwch, Pentre Galar; SN 17323249: There are now only very faint traces of the circular cairn here, which are very hard to see.

54. Pentre Galar; SN 17233072: Site of the TV mast, on top of a cairn. This had already been demolished as a source of hardcore for the main road; records indicate that it may have had a cist in it. An axe-hammer recorded in 1927 appears to have come from the cairn, and could have been used in its construction. This is possibly another wayside cairn, linked to the Glandy Cross complex at the south-west end of the hill. There are no visible remains, but it is perhaps worth going up to the mast from Pentre-Galar hamlet to see the position of the site. Of the two cairns known as Crugiau Dwy, at SN 17143115, only one remains, and that in a very dilapidated state. It is in rough pasture in the extreme south-east corner of the enclosed hillside north-east of Penyddafad farm, just over the stone wall which

BRONZE AGE SITES: 2500-1400 BC

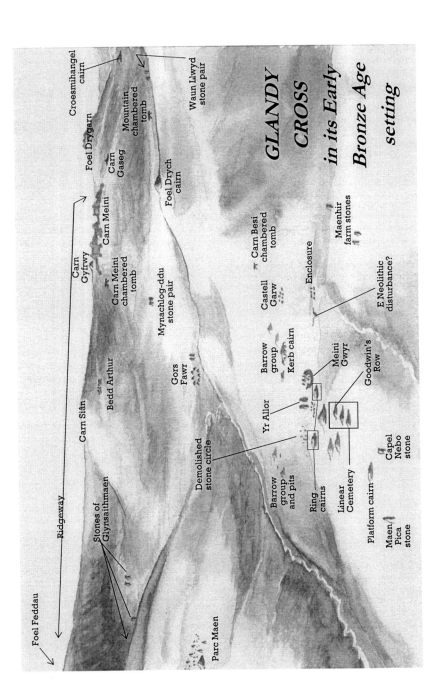

GLANDY CROSS in its Early Bronze Age setting

Foel Feddau

Ridgeway

Stones of Glynsaithmaen

Parc Maen

Carn Siân

Bedd Arthur

Carn Gyfrwy

Carn Meini

Carn Meini chambered tomb

Mynachlog-ddu stone pair

Cors Fawr

Foel Drygarn

Carn Gaseg

Mountain chambered tomb

Croesmihangel cairn

Foel Drych cairn

Waun Llwyd stone pair

Carn Besi chambered tomb

Castell Garw

Enclosure

Maenhir farm stones

E Neolithic disturbance?

Barrow group

Kerb cairn

Yr Allor

Demolished stone circle

Meini Gwyr

Goodwin's Row

Barrow group and pits

Ring cairns

Linear Cemetery

Capel Nebo stone

Platform cairn

Maen Pica stone

divides that pasture from Penyddafad pasture, but not accessible from the TV mast. A long walk for small reward!

55. Foel Dyrch, Pentre Galar hill; SN 15943004: This was once a large cairn, but a sheepfold built in its midriff has rather altered its appearance! It can be reached uphill from the lane immediately north of Trefach on the Glandy Cross/ Mynachlog-ddu road. The longer walk up from Penyddafad farm on the Pentre Galar/Mynachlog-ddu road gives really marvellous views of the positions of all the hill-top cairns of the east Preselis and Pentre Galar hill, and is well worth the extra time it takes.

56. Glandy Cross Complex

The Glandy Cross Prehistoric Complex is the least known and most important gathering of 'ritual' sites in West Wales, and one of the most significant along the whole length of the British west coast. It was unexplored until recently, by which time many of its monuments had been either ploughed down or thrown down in the course of land-improvement and building. This is the result of historical inevitability; good land is scarce so close to the mountains, and where there are farms it is the way of settlements to sprout. Visually, Glandy Cross is perhaps disappointing; other than Meini Gwyr (see below) most of what is here is either hard to see or actually invisible, but with the aid of a picture-map it is hoped that something of this extraordinary ritual landscape may be recreated in the mind's eye. Taking it as accepted that cursus monuments were very early, it has always seemed likely that the first sites in the area were the axe-flaking sites on the east slope of Pentre Galar and at Yr Allor, the Llandissilio cursus (if confirmed - see below), and the passage-grave type chambered tombs. There are four of these: at Mountain, at the headwaters of the Cleddau; on Carn Meini; at Carn Besi (not far from the axe site), and at Gwal-y-Filiast on the Taf, east of our area. Very recently a radio-carbon date obtained from a hollow near Pantymenyn has given a reading from the Early Neolithic - around 4300 BC. If it applies to human activities, it would be the earliest sign of Neolithic communities in Preseli (although late Mesolithic people or natural 'bush-fires' might equally have been responsible). It has always seemed slightly odd that Preseli, sticking right out into the sea-roads travelled by Early Neolithic settlers, should have been ignored by them. Perhaps it wasn't? The large-scale setting for this early date is not yet known, but it may signal the presence of human activity in this significant area before even the axe-making tradition was developed - or may be relevant to the inauguration of axe-making in an area rich in suitable stone. It has been suggested that there may be a connexion in Wales between cursus monuments and axe dissemination, and between this and river-ways; if so, these factors may contribute to the hypothesis that there was a cursus at the point where the Cleddau comes closest to a north-south trans-peninsular track. Henges also have very early origins and again, in Wales, have been linked with axe-production. The site at Castell Garw, thought to have been a henge, has recently been investigated and discovered to be a Late Bronze Age/Early Iron Age defensive site, but activity there before the banks were constructed may be very much older - possibly contemporary with the funerary complex. The denuded earthwork at **Pantymenyn, SN 148263**, another 'henge' candidate, has turned out to be a linear enclosure, and pits investigated there and close to Yr Allor have only served to add to the impression of intense, complicated ritual activity right across the area. At the time of writing, there would seem to be no likely henge site in the Glandy Cross area - an interesting absence.

Meini Gwyr, SN 14172658, is the only site in the complex which invites the public. The Dyfed Archaeological Trust (DAT) has provided an excellent

BRONZE AGE SITES: 2500-1400 BC

explanatory board at the entrance, complete with reconstruction drawings, a history of the site and a map of other sites in the Glandy Cross Complex. The monument now consists only of the remains of the bank and two of the original seventeen stones.

Meini Gwyr is an 'embanked stone circle', a type that seems to the modern eye to have something of the henge, something of the stone circle and something of the ring-barrow invested in its design. However, since we do not know how stone circles or henges were used, the resemblance may not be a real one. The circle seems to have been used over a period of time, but how long is not clear. On the side opposite the entrance there was a hearth in a hollow on the bank. It has been suggested that the hollow was the setting for a stone no longer there, and that the monument was therefore altered at some time in its functional life. In the hearth were fragments of Food Vessel pottery, a style current from about 2300 BC onwards elsewhere. This gives a vicarious date for activity at Meini Gwyr - 2300 BC or later. If there was any time-lapse between the original creation of the hollow and the setting of the fire in it, then the life-span of the bank, at least, must have begun earlier - but maybe only by long enough for the designers to change the plan!

The most that can be said is that Meini Gwyr was almost certainly designed for specific ceremonial activities, and that many Neolithic and Early Bronze Age ceremonies do seem to have included contact with the dead, frequently involving the burial or re-burial of cremated bone fragments. Whether these bits of the dead hallowed the place, or the place hallowed the dead, archaeology cannot reveal. In fact, the 1938 excavation recovered no signs of the dead. A pit in front of the entrance contained much charcoal, but without indication of what the fire may have been for (oak charcoal, for example, indicates a funeral pyre because of its fierce burning quality).

One interesting discovery was the fact that the seventeen stones set against the bank were leaning inwards. Leaning stones are not necessarily collapsing; there are several cases where the angle is part of the original design (see **81**), and it seems that the stones surrounding some of the stone-encircled barrows (e.g. **33**) were set

Impression of Meini Gwyr as it may have been. In high summer the setting sun shines inwards into the circle through the entrance.

to lean outwards. To us, to-day, an outward tilt seems to imply release (akin to opening the window at a death to release the soul), and an inward tilt containment. DAT's reconstruction drawing captures the secretive atmosphere and the sense of enclosure with which the stone-lined entrance and oppressive angle of the stones must originally have endowed Meini Gwyr.

Yr Allor: Standing stones two fields west of Meini Gwyr. Quite definite records of there having been three stones here, where now there are only two, put this monument out of the paired stones category. Investigations have shown that the leaning stone was deliberately propped that way, which undermines the idea that Yr Allor might have been a 'cove' - curious arrangements like a three-sided stall, the most famous of which is at Avebury inside one of the stone circles. It seems unlikely that a cove would incorporate a leaning stone. An area of cobbling and some Early Bronze Age pits were found around the two stones, so they were certainly the focus of activity at quite a late date. Nearby were found a number of stone flakes struck off in the process of shaping Neolithic stone axes. While the majority of stone axes were obviously everyday tools, some certainly had symbolic value as well, so perhaps the stones at Yr Allor originally had something to do with the non-functional aspect of axes. Although most of the standing stones seem to date from the Early Bronze Age, several centuries later than the axe-manufacturing sites, the two need not necessarily be widely separated in time; the time-bracket within which standing stones were erected is very wide, and some have been proved to be of very early origin.

There is another axe-manufacturing site to the north (**15**). Since, taken overall, the early monuments Glandy Cross do seem to have a hypothetical connexion with axe-making, it appears that the area may owe some of its original mystique to the ritual side of axe-creation. However, this connexion between axes and early sites of the henge and cursus type is not sustained everywhere, and it may simply be that incomplete evidence has produced a distorted picture at Glandy Cross as we know it now.

Early descriptions of the stones around Yr Allor and Meini Gwyr suggest that there was another stone circle (which might mean something like Gors Fawr, or like Meini Gwyr, or a stone kerb of a demolished barrow). One record implies a second 'cove'-like arrangement near the main road. This latter may be a confusion with Yr Allor itself, but even if so, the density of monuments is remarkable. No wonder that such a place became a focus for the elaborate burial practices of the next generations, whose barrows surround the stones and Meini Gwyr. The largest of these can be seen in the field south of Meini Gwyr as a grassy mound, and the information board at the site gate shows where others were.

Only a part of one of these has been excavated, **Goodwin's Row barrow**, which is now built over and invisible. Here the original core of the barrow had already been demolished by the building of the road, but enough of it was left to show that the turf had been stripped off before the barrow was begun. This may have been to provide a 'floor' for whatever rituals (dance, circular processions?) took place at the time of the initial burial. This original burial had already been demolished by the road, and all that remained was a low mound of quartz stones which presumably covered it. The quartz was surrounded by a kerb of low, upright stones which became unsteady and were later secured by stakes. After some years it was all covered by a layer of thick turves, apparently laid upside down (no question here of an imitation 'natural' hillock) with a fresh, larger kerb of boulders running round it, all of which could have been collected from the immediate vicinity. Later still, the now rather grand barrow was enlarged by adding a layer of clay behind and outside the kerb so that the whole thing spread out further. At some point - there was not enough detail left to be sure when - a pavement of white quartz was laid at the side

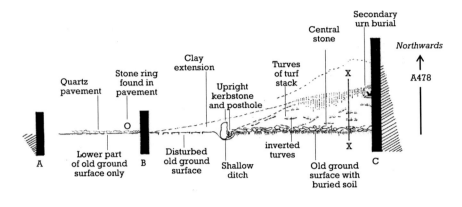

Diagram of structural sequence at Goodwin's Row barrow.

Only a quarter of this barrow remained to be studied in 1987-8 when the site was proposed for building development. The excavation extracted the maximum amount of information from the minimum of material.

The thick black columns show where modern activities interfered with the interpretation of the remains: A. Recent trackway; B. Recent garden plot obscuring the only place where the relationship between the mound edge and the quartz pavement might have been clarified; C. Turnpike road, now A748, dug through and obliterating the primary deposit.

X is the relative position of one of the environmental columns which retrieved the pollen record.

This is a representative diagram, not an actual section. (Based on Murphy, 1990.)

of the kerb. This has been related in some detail because it shows that at each enlargement or alteration the mound was kept bare, or even made more obvious by the use of pale stones. It was meant to be blatant in the landscape. Finally the cremated remains of a young adult were buried in an urn which was placed in a stone cist at the top of the mound. This time the urn was the right way up, and also held the oak charcoal from the pyre. Pieces of stone appropriate to cists were found in the road-making debris, so there may have been more cremations which used the original barrow. Fragments of another urn were found a century ago - it is not clear whether in this barrow or its neighbour - and three stone beads turned up in the garden top-soil of an adjacent house.

The other barrows have not been excavated, but the sequence of care and 'improvements' expended on Goodwin's Row shows how the Glandy Cross cemetery was kept over generations as a landscape which looked different, special, and outside the usual green pastoral environs. Analysis of the pollen of the plants growing when the barrow was built shows that even then the area was a sort of scrubby heathland, the woodland already long gone but meadows not developed; the sort of vegetation of a place much used but set apart from everyday economics. It need not be imagined as drear, with a number of bald tumps like fresh mole-hills scattered across it. There is no evidence for dyed flags on tall poles set up on the mounds, for swinging wind-bells, 'bone-trees', painted stones or posts. None of these would leave any mark (except stake-holes, and there are always plenty of them).

Goodwin's Row is one of several barrows (of which some seemed to have flat rather than dome-shaped tops) running in a string south from Glandy Cross. The largest of these can be seen as a grassy mound in the field immediately south of Meini Gwyr, with the subdued silhouette of a ring cairn just to its left. The bigger mound is peculiarly shaped and may be a composite structure like a ring or circle set upon a platform, something quite out of the ordinary. There is another group on the north side of Glandy Cross, running uphill behind the pub. One of these seems to have been of exceptional importance; the platform is kerbed with unusually heavy stones, so that it has sometimes been mistaken for a stone circle (cf. **33**). A hedge has cut off some of it, and brambles have swallowed the interior. There are still more barrows, indistinguishable now, around Yr Allor and out to the east. The DAT Information board at Meini Gwyr shows how many of these are ring-barrows rather than the less specialised round-barrows.

Apart from the two stones left at Yr Allor, the standing stones of the area are set around the periphery, as if whatever statement they are making was collateral rather than germane to the developing cemetery. Not included in the gazetteer of standing stones (*below*) are two possible stones between the cursus and Capel Nebo, and two more, out to the east of Glandy Cross, marked on the board.

57. Lan barrow; SN 132250: Newly discovered signs that there was a barrow here, just south of Maen Pica standing stone, extends the Glandy Cross funerary complex southwards. There is no access, and no visible remains.

58. Garnwen; SN 169288: A number of urns were found around here in the 19th century. One contained cremated bone, but unfortunately all have been lost. It is possibly somewhere in this area that one of the Early Bronze Age flat-axes was found (see p. 29), suggesting that this whole area below and including Pentre Galar hill was involved in the intense activity of which the Glandy Cross complex is the visible legacy.

59. Rhos Coynant; SN 15382549: The site has now been levelled and there is nothing to see, but the recorded position of a barrow here among the standing stones calls to mind the multi-phase site at Parc Maen (**42**), across the Cleddau.

60. A.Taf; SN 186273: A number of 'urns' found here at the beginning of the 20th century were thought to be Roman and consequently(!) thrown away. This is slightly outside our area, but the find is an interesting sequitur to the urn burials recorded north of these on the opposite bank of the Taf (**58**).

*

BRONZE AGE SITES:
2500-1400 BC

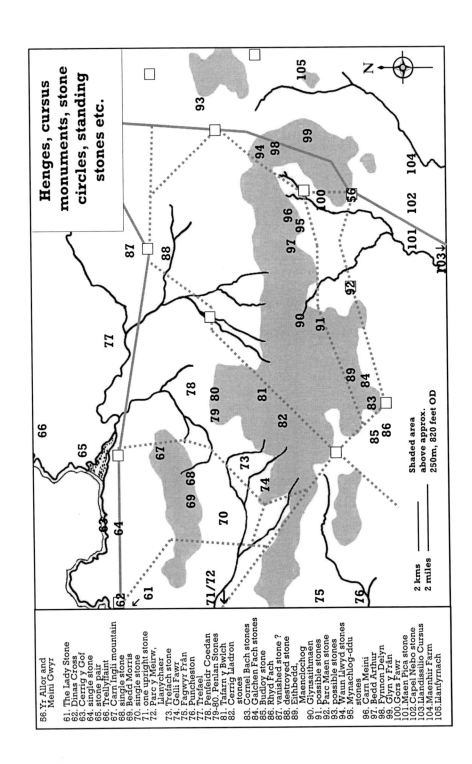

Henges, cursus monuments, stone circles, standing stones etc.

56. Yr Allor and
     Meini Gwyr

61. The Lady Stone
62. Dinas Cross
63. Cerrig y Gof
64. single stone
65. stone pair
66. Trellyffaint
67. Carn Ingli mountain
68. single stone
69. Bedd Morris
70. single stone
71. one upright stone
72. Parc y Meirw,
     Llanychaer
73. Trefach stone
74. Gelli Fawr
75. Fagwyr Frân
76. Puncheston
77. Trefael
78. Penfeidr Coedan
79-80. Penlan Stones
81. Tafarn y Bwlch
82. Cerrig Lladron
     stones
83. Cornel Bach stones
84. Galchen Fach stones
85. Budloy stone
86. Rhyd Fach
87. vanished stone ?
88. destroyed stone
89. Eithbedd,
     Maenclochog
90. Glynsaithmaen
91. possible stones
92. Parc Maen stone
93. possible stones
94. Waun Llwyd stones
95. Mynachlog-ddu
     stones
96. Carn Meini
97. Bedd Arthur
98. Fynnon Delyn
99. Glyn y Frân
100. Gors Fawr
101. Maen Pica stone
102. Capel Nebo stone
103. Llandissilio Cursus
104. Maenhir Farm
105. Llanfyrnach

Shaded area
above approx.
250m, 820 feet OD

2 kms
2 miles

HENGES, CURSUS MONUMENTS,
STONE CIRCLES, STANDING STONES etc.

Many of these 'ritual' monuments have burials associated with them, but they are usually distinguished in the literature, as the current view is that this was not their primary function. Henges and cursus monuments are probably the earliest; standing stones continued to be raised over perhaps fifteen centuries.

61. The Lady Stone; SM 99573762: So called because it looks like a cloaked woman - travellers on the old Fishguard coaches regularly doffed their hats to her. From the other side of the road, a couple of yards towards Fishguard, she bears an uncanny resemblance to a certain Scottish widow.

62. Dinas Cross; SN 00813875: In the field immediately beyond the motor repair works at the end of the village, on the north side of the main road. Visible from the road.

63. Cerrig y Gof; SN 03563892: A recumbent stone west of and in the same field as the chambered tomb (3). Pitted, thought by some to be cup-marked.

64. Single stone; SN 040393: Small, no access.

65. Stone pair; SN 067410: On the east side of the road, half way between Wynston and Pen-cnwc-isaf farms. The stone still in use as a gatepost may have been pecked; the other has been felled, and is in the hedgerow immediately behind it.

66. Trellyffaint; SN 08294230: A single stone, which may be natural, near the chambered tomb (2).

67. Carn Ingli mountain; SN 06173785: A single undistinguished stone amongst round barrows (?) or hut-circles (see **24**).

68. Single stone; SN 04733631: One of a number of deceptive stones which are probably cattle-rubs.

69. Bedd Morris; SN 03823650: Not mentioned by early antiquaries, so this handsome stone may be a modern boundary stone.

70. Single stone; SN 007356: Damaged, no access.

71. SN 001358: One upright stone of pair. No access.

72. Parc y Meirw, Llanychaer; Stone Row; SM 99883591: A magnificent alignment of huge monoliths running west-south-west/east-north-east on high ground above the right bank of the Gwaun. The stones are now deeply embedded in the bank of a very narrow, sunken road. The four stones still erect are best seen by standing right in the gateway of which two of the stones now form superlative 'portals', and looking at the field-side of the bank, where their true height and grandeur can be appreciated. There were eight stones here in the 19th century. Two of the missing ones are visible from the road in the bank to the west of the standing

**BRONZE AGE SITES:
2500-1400 BC**

stones, the remainder are probably part of the structure of the bank itself. This is the only long stone alignment of this height and grandeur in West Wales and, when entire, would have compared well with the more famous alignments of Argyll or Orkney. The name means 'The Place of the Dead', and is taken to refer to a peculiarly bloody early mediaeval battle said to have been fought here on a field between the sea and Carn Ingli mountain. The depth of the roadway below the stones shows that they have been used as a way-marker for many centuries. Just east of the row a single stone has been moved and laid on top of the wall by Trellwyn Farm. From the east side of the yard an unsignposted track runs down past Trellwyn Fach to the Gwaun. A damaged stone was found in the field immediately west of this farm.

The three eastern-most stones of Parc y Meirw. Two have been used as a modern gatepost; a fourth lies west of these in the roadside bank.

73. Trefach stone; SN 06403505: A fine pointed stone which may be part of the collapsed chambered tomb a few yards away (7). Visible from the road.

74. Gelli Fawr; SN 06153444: A possible single stone.

75. Fagwyr Frân; SN 00483145: A single, triangular stone, which can be seen from the road. A possible stone row just to the north-west is not visible.

76. Puncheston; SN 00953025: A magnificent broad-faced stone, well worth seeing - one of the best! Visible through the field gate beside the passing place immediately north of the white house on the Fagwr Frân/Puncheston road, about 450 yards north of Puncheston. A second separate stone has been re-housed in a garden in the village, and cannot be seen.

77. Trefael; SN 10294028: A single stone, tilting, cup marked (see 2). There is no direct access but the stone is visible across the field from the footpath.

78. Penfeidr Coedan; SN 09923688: An impressive line of naturally vertical strata, thought to be perhaps the source of Pentre Ifan stone (see 8). The pointed, western stone is possibly a standing stone. There is no access, but the ridge is visible from the road near the cottage immediately to the south

79-80. Penlan stones: No access, but all are visible from roadside banks and gaps. **SN 09023573**: Dramatically isolated pair in the middle of a field; **SN 09043543**: A single stone against the hedge on the other side of the road.

81. Tafarn y Bwlch stone complex; c.SN 081337: An exciting moorland site with easy open access. It is possible to park by the cattle-grid.
A. A stone pair, more likely to be a genuine pair than part of a collapsed chambered tomb, as has sometimes been suggested. Leaning stones are not unknown in Preseli, and the angle of these is carefully matched. These stones are at a short distance slightly

to the left and below the track leading north-west from the cattle-grid.

B. A larger single stone, further along the same track but on the right.

C. A group of stones, variously considered as a pair with one stone fallen, a group with more than one fallen and - least likely - remnants of a circle of which most are fallen. No early references or place names suggest the former presence of a circle; the three stones involved would indicate an enormous diameter. Interpretation open to suggestions! The stones cannot be seen from B, but are just over the shoulder of the hill. From B strike approximately north-east across the hill (there is no path) towards the fence dividing the fields from the unenclosed moorland.

Another boulder on the east side of the road leading southwards from the cattle-grid is now thought to be natural, but has been considered as a further standing-stone.

Paired stones at Tafarn y Bwlch, leaning to the north.

82. Cerrig Lladron stones; SN 06673229: Two stones unevenly matched, so possibly not a pair. Unusually high up on the mountain.

83. Cornel Bach stones; SN 08142777 & 08162778: Two separate stones in a field, visible from the right side of the unmetalled lane to the right of the last houses on the north side of Maenclochog village.

84. Galchen Fach stones; SN 08752780: A stone pair; no access, but visible from the road-bank above the bridge.

85. Budloy stone; SN 066285: A magisterial, tall single stone in a field above the left bank of the A. Syfynwy. The marked footpath which passes Dyffryn Syfynwy ring-cairn (**33**) affords fine views of the stone from afar, and passes close beside it.

86. Rhyd Fach; SN 066282: Single stone. Not visible, no access.

87. SN 164397: Documentary evidence suggests that there was once a stone here. If so, this extends distribution.

88. SN 136380: There was once a single stone here, known to have been dynamited in the 19th century.

89. Eithbedd, Maenclochog; SN 092292 : Early antiquarians' records show that as recently as the end of the 19th century there was a stone circle in the Eithbedd area, at Maen Llwyd Farm. There are no remains left, but it is interesting that there was a circle here quite distinct from the many monuments in the Gors-Fawr/ Glandy Cross area.

There is also a circular embankment of considerable size at the bottom of the field where the stones from the demolished chambered tombs have been piled (see **12**). The possibility that it may be a henge, rather than an Iron Age defensive bank, is made marginally greater by its position so close to the tombs.

BRONZE AGE SITES: 2500-1400 BC

90. Glynsaithmaen stone complex; centred on SN 115305: The name suggests either seven stones or particular stones traditionally potent for arrow-sharpening. The group includes:

A. Stones of the Sons of Arthur. A fine stone pair accessible across the moor from the unfenced road west of Glynsaithmaen farm. (See front cover.) They are named after the 'sons' of Arthur killed here in the Hunt for the Great Boar as told in *Culhwch and Olwen* in the *Mabinogion*.

B. A single stone in the field bank of the paddock near the house. Not accessible.

C. Possibly a prostrate stone in the farmyard. Not visible.

D. A single stone on the inside of the hedge beside the road to the south-west of the farm. It is difficult to see, but this can just be done by climbing on to the road-bank.

E. A single stone visible in a field belonging to Gate Farm, west across the road from D.

The Stones of Glynsaithmaen

Above, left: *Stone in home paddock* (B); Right: *Stone on field side of roadside bank* (D).

Left: *Gate Farm stone, visible from roadbank* (E).

This makes six stones in all. Other large monoliths in and around the farm and track behind A have been mooted as the seventh. None is indisputable. This is a remarkable collection gathered around the hollow of the hills, indicating that Glynsaithmaen must have been a special place of considerable significance. There is nothing to show whether all the stones were erected at the same time or whether the presence of one or two attracted others. The modern stone at the farm gate is a memorial to a local poet/historian and bard who lived here, and is a beautiful example of polished bluestone.

91. SN 089290 & 114286: Possible single stones; **SN 098288**: Possible pair.

92. Parc Maen stone; SN 113283: See **42.** The stone, which is quite a small one, can be seen in an enclosed field by taking the bridlepath running west opposite Spring Gardens Cottage. At the young ash tree strike north into the brambles, surmount the first bank and stand on the next (field-boundary) bank. Uncomfortable, but interesting for the dedicated to see the site of such an important excavation!

93. At SN 193370 & 193372: Two separate possible stones, extending distribution if valid. No access.

94. Waun Llwyd stones; SN 15773126: A magnificent stone pair on the east of the Cleddau upwaters. Visit only with permission from the farm. The stones can also be seen at a distance from Mountain chambered tomb **(14)**.

95. Mynachlog-ddu stones; SN 13433048: A small stone pair in the field beyond the north edge of the common; visible from the bank behind the Bluestone Memorial Stone. A putative third stone is no longer distinguishable.

96. Carn Meini; SN 145325: Natural, or perhaps not quite so natural, outcrop. The most spectacular of the rocky crags from which the Stonehenge bluestones are said to have been taken (see pp. 47-51).

97. Bedd Arthur; SN 13053250: This peculiar stone setting appears sparsely in the records, because no one is quite sure what it is. Physically, it is a set of thirteen or so small, obviously upstanding stones, and two or three more, now semi-buried,

Photograph: Ailinor Evans

The inscrutable stones of Bedd Arthur, with Carn Meini behind.

BRONZE AGE SITES:
2500-1400 BC

which may be part of it. Faint traces of what may have been a bank are visible, especially on the long north side. It appears to have been deliberately flattened inside, and a hollow in the centre could be contemporary. Most records now include it as '?hengiform', on the assumption that it must be prehistoric; and a stone circle, or henge with a stone circle, is what it most nearly resembles. It is less likely to be a Viking boat-grave or a neo-Druidical prank. The site is spectacular - directly across the stone-river from Carn Meini, on a flat natural terrace under Carn Arthur crags. Taking it as some form of stone 'circle', some have drawn it with a dotted line joining the stones into an oval, others as quite a severe rectangle. There are rectangular monuments throughout the henge/stone-circle period, but they are rare. Bedd Arthur is aligned east-north-east/west-south-west, within the range common for henges and circles, and athwart the natural contours as well as diagonally to Carn Meini - which would militate against Carn Meini's being its *raison d'être*. As an aside, it may be imaginatively piquant to note that there is another stone rectangle, rather better known than this one. (See p. 51.)

The name means 'The Grave of Arthur'. Contrary to popular impressions, while there are lots of stones, tables, woods, quoits, bawns and caves, there are very few 'graves' of Arthur. The strong Arthurian connexion with Preseli is found in the *Mabinogion*, a collection of mediaeval Welsh tales. Some of these may have extremely ancient origins, and one certainly gave rise to the name of the standing stone pair (**90A**) on the bog below. Bedd Arthur may well have taken its name from theirs, since its outline is not unlike that of a singularly large grave. That it might have acquired its name not from of the proximity of the stones, but from the same arcane source, is another remote possibility.

Altogether, Bedd Arthur is an eerie site, with big question marks hanging over its origin.

98. Ffynnon Delyn; SN 178303: Possible henge site. Not visible, not confirmed.

99. Glyn y Frân; SN 185307: Probable ritual complex near axe-manufacturing site. Not visible, no access.

100. Gors Fawr; SN 1346 2937: A stone circle, the only true stone circle left in Preseli. (See the photograph on page 32.) It stands on open moorland, with public access and parking, just south of Mynachlog-ddu. This is small as places like Avebury go, but typical of western Britain and Ireland. The sixteen stones are all small, the highest merely 2ft high, and mostly fairly squat. They are of spotted ('bluestone'-type) dolerite, unspotted dolerite and undetermined rock, all of which occur as local erratics. The fact that the stones increase in height towards the south-west has given rise to comparisons with a Dartmoor stone-circle. The circle they form is not quite exact. Some stone circles are so 'egg-shaped' that they have been recorded in a 'sub-category' of stone circles, but Gors Fawr is only slightly off a true circle.

At the beginning of the 20th century an 'Avenue' was said to lead from the circle to the two outlying standing stones to the north-north-east. There are so many boulders lying around on the common that it is impossible to conjecture which are the ones involved, but it is certainly true that there may well be formations or emplacements of stones concealed in what appears to be a random scatter. The two outliers, a fine pair of standing stones, each 2m high, are at an angle apparently offset from the circle. This has led to the suggestion that they may not be 'outliers' in any true sense, and that their relationship to the circle may be indirect. They are both of bluestone, but of somewhat different forms. It is possible to look through them to the site of the paired stones in the bog at Glynsaithmaen (**90A**), and through those to the saddle between Carn Sian and Foel Feddau. On a straight line directly beyond the Glynsaithmaen stones, out of sight on the other side of the mountain, is the complex at Tafarn y Bwlch (**81**), which also includes a stone pair and a possible (doubtful?) stone circle. This sort of map-created linkage has given rise to all manner of theories on the function and meaning of standing stones, but it is possible to draw lines in all directions if it is not known what they are lines of, or what has been lost in the surrounding landscape. Pending the invention of some economically viable method of verifying the geo-physics involved in the placement of all standing, fallen, demolished, moved, lost and undiscovered stones, any of these linear interpretations is at best an artifact of modern fancy. This does not mean that one such theory may not turn out to be true - archaeology has a habit of confounding the sceptic!

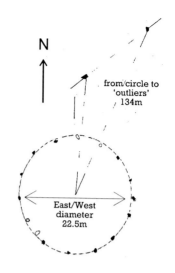

Gors Fawr circle. Upstanding stones are shown black, fallen and submerged stones are shown open, The two 'outliers' are illustrated at their relative compass positions. (After Burl, 1985.)

101. Maen Pica stone; SN 13172523: A fine single stone. The pointed top is broken. No access. The stone is just visible over a hedge from the farm gateway.

102. Capel Nebo stone; SN 13852540: A fine, squarish single stone. It is visible from the road-bank, directly across the field south of the chapel, as a bulky gatepost.

103. Llandissilio Cursus; SN 119215-126212: Aerial photography picked up a double line of cropmarks 15-20m apart, running for about 700m in an east-west direction under Llandissilio village, 3½ miles (5½ km) south of Meini Gwyr. There are indications that at one end there may be internal features and a cross-ditch. There is nothing visible on the ground. Cursus monuments were so called because they reminded early antiquarians of race-tracks, and may indeed be processional ways (perhaps for special axes, or whatever special axes signified), although recently both funerary and territorial functions have been suggested for them. Again, this putative monument is a recent discovery and has not been confirmed by excavation; it may yet turn out to be something much less ancient! If it is a cursus, it would emphasise the great antiquity of this landscape as a special place. The position of the crop-mark, near the river and in the same area as both a henge and axe-making activities, is typical of known cursus monuments, and bodes well for its future verification.

104. Maenhir Farm (and close by); SN 155255: A group of single stones, three of which are visible from the road. From the third field-gate from the T junction one can be seen near the right side of the field, and another behind it in the hedge. (These two have sometimes been quoted as the remnants of a dismantled chambered tomb - see **19**). A third is immediately behind the telegraph pole on the

BRONZE AGE SITES: 2500-1400 BC

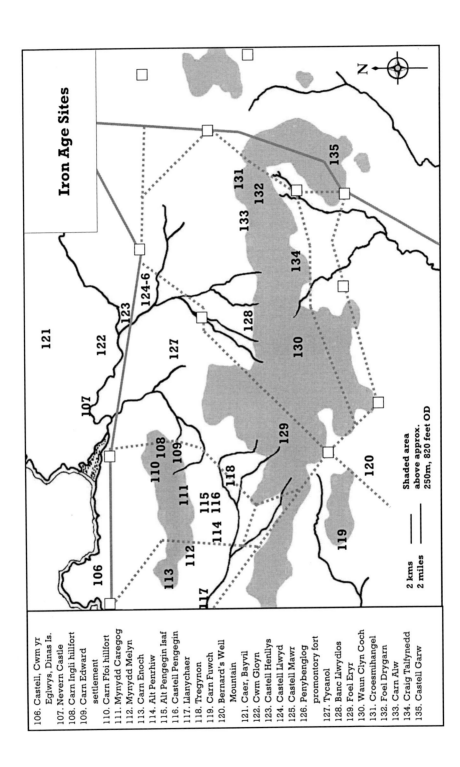

Iron Age Sites

N

106. Castell, Cwm yr
     Eglwys, Dinas Is.
107. Nevern Castle
108. Carn Ingli hillfort
109. Carn Edward
     settlement
110. Carn Ffoi hillfort
111. Mynydd Caregog
112. Mynydd Melyn
113. Carn Enoch
114. Alt Penrhiw
115. Alt Pengegin Isaf
116. Castell Pengegin
117. Llanychaer
118. Tregynon
119. Carn Fuwch
120. Bernard's Well
     Mountain
121. Caer, Bayvil
122. Cwm Gloyn
123. Castell Henllys
124. Castell Llwyd
125. Castell Mawr
126. Penybenglog
     promontory fort
127. Tycanol
128. Banc Llwydlos
129. Foel Eryr
130. Waun Clyn Coch
131. Croesmihangel
132. Foel Drygarn
133. Carn Alw
134. Craig Talfynedd
135. Castell Garw

Shaded area
above approx.
250m, 820 feet OD

2 kms
2 miles

right of the entrance to Maenhir Farm, and can almost be seen from the cattle-grid! The fourth is up by the farm buildings, which are private.

105. Llanfyrnach: Outside the area. There have been a number of stones around here, some of which have been removed from valuable pasture.

The last group (101-4) are interesting as an extension of the complex at Glandy Cross. See also **59**.

Note.

An eighteenth-century record notes 'near Kily-Maen-Llwyd on a great mountain a circle of mighty stones very much like Stonehenge in Wiltshire, or rather like the Rollrych Stones in Oxfordshire'. The whereabouts of this demolished circle is unknown. Cilmaenllwyd parish includes Glandy Cross, but no 'great mountain'.

Yr Allor and Meini Gwyr frequently appear in older descriptions and maps as pairs of standing stones. However, see **56**.

IRON AGE SITES

This section of the Gazetteer includes only sites which are visible on the ground, and a couple of significant areas of landscape where important sites have been recorded which are either not visible, or have no public access. There are over seventy recorded Iron Age locations in Preseli, of which the great majority cannot be visited, and some of which can be seen only from the air!

106. Castell, Cwm yr Eglwys, Dinas Is.; SN 01344019: A possible hillfort/ promontory fort site near the coastal path. A spindle whorl (now in Scolton Museum) was found in the sea wall at Cwm yr Eglwys, and some undated flints have been collected from nearby. This is one of several sites possibly fortified in the Iron Age, none of which is securely dated. The proximity of finds on this side of the island suggests that this is more likely to be a prehistoric site than either of the others.

107. Nevern Castle; SN 082481: There is an Iron Age site beneath the mediaeval castle. Nothing prehistoric is visible.

108. Carn Ingli mountain, Carn Ingli hillfort; SN 063373:
A formidable, single-rampart fortification surrounding jagged and inhospitable crags, with remains of hut emplacements and terraces. (See the picture on the back cover.) It must be said at the outset that any exploration of the interior of the hillfort is not for the faint-hearted. The ground is boulder-strewn, unsteady in parts, steep, and in summer covered with deceptive bracken. However, the main entrance and some of the better preserved walling are quite easily approachable from the gentle western side facing Carn Briw. For the vigorous, the interior and the surrounding wall-work are breath-taking, in both senses.

IRON AGE SITES:
800 BC - AD56

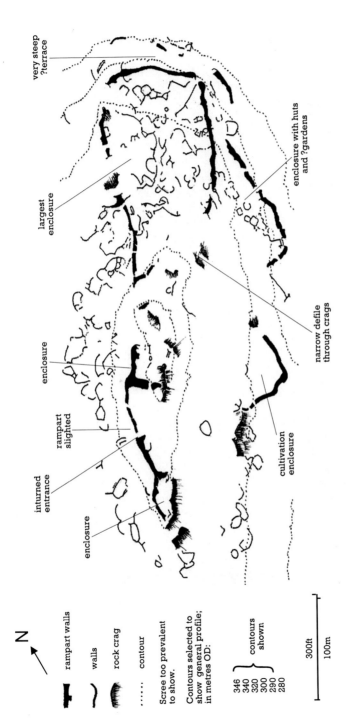

Carn Ingli hillfort.

(After Hogg, 1973.)

N

very steep
?terrace

largest
enclosure

enclosure with huts
and ?gardens

enclosure

rampart
slighted

narrow defile
through crags

inturned
entrance

enclosure

cultivation
enclosure

rampart walls

walls

rock crag

contour

Scree too prevalent
to show.

Contours selected to
show general profile;
in metres OD:

346
340
320
300   } contours
290   shown
280

300ft

100m

The hillfort is a series of conjoined enclosures encompassed by a massive stone wall, with huts and cultivation plots inside and a sprawl of expanded terraces outside. It is thought that the central, highest enclosure may be the earliest, and that the comfortless and equally defensible annexe on the north, and the much gentler enclosures on the south, were subsequent developments. The earliest enclosure seems to have been constructed to use the massive central crag to full defensive advantage, and the same could be true of the northern annexe with its sheer rocks. At the same time, both these areas seem so uneven, cramped and spartan that they must have been built to counter some real danger, whereas the less tumultuous areas to the south and east might well have fulfilled a less confrontational rôle. Nonetheless, there is evidence that lengths of the defences were slighted, although it is not known when. The eastern enclosures may be individual settlement areas or cultivation terraces like those opposite on the gentle western slope. The rectangular shapes of some of the hut-foundations have led to a tentative inquiry as to whether the northern and eastern enclosures may not have had much older origins, and incorporate remains of Neolithic defences such as are found on other fortified-crag sites in western Britain (e.g. Clegyr Boia in south Pembrokeshire and Carn Brea in Cornwall - see p. 25). It has also been suggested that the proximity of field-systems, hut circles and monuments of Bronze Age date on the mountain might indicate that Carn Ingli was one of several sites fortified in the late Bronze Age. Since there is no dating evidence available, all these progenitors are possible, as are the alternative theories that the whole complex was initially Iron Age and that the storming of the walls may have been due to a Roman offensive, or that the fort continued in use until early mediaeval times and was taken during that violent age.

The hut circle/enclosure and field-system at SN 05253715 are most easily found in low light and low vegetation, near the track down to Carn Ffoi. Another track running downhill due north from the hillfort passes an excellently preserved hut-circle (one of several close together at c. SN063378) immediately south of the crossing of this path with the east/west path. (See **24** and **67**.)

109. A. Carn Edward settlement, SN0549 3681: Three annular structures easily found two-thirds of the way down the hill-slope just to the south of a straight line between Carn Briw cairn and Carn Edward outcrop. Authorities are divided as to whether these are ring-cairns (**26**) or hut foundations.
B. Carn Llwyd open settlement, SN 054369: A number of circular enclosures, some of which may be ring-cairns, others homesteads, and which are taken to include probable Bronze Age settlement.
C. Waun Fawr; SN 049375: A system of small fields and paddocks interspersed with what may be clearance cairns. To the west of the path between Carn Briw and Carn Ffoi; easier to see in winter.

> *A number of other field-systems and possible settlement sites which may have a Bronze Age origin are to be found on Carn Ingli. The dating of many of them is uncertain, and the distinction between 'late Bronze Age' and 'Iron Age' is not really applicable here. Carn Ingli mountain attracted monuments and settlements over millennia, and their occupation and use will inevitably have overlapped and merged in time and space. Only the most visible are listed above.*

110. Carn Ffoi hillfort; SN 048379: Almost exactly a mile north-west and below Carn Ingli hillfort, but overlooking a distinctly separate area. Since neither hillfort is dated, nothing is known about their relationship. Carn Ffoi is a small, essentially simple structure not unlike Carn Alw (**133**). A single stone wall joins three rocky outcrops to south, east and north, and

**IRON AGE SITES:
800 BC - AD56**

Carn Ffoi. The faint outlines of prehistoric hut circles can be picked out among the fallen rampart stones.

runs round the rim of a steep slope to the west. The interior is relatively flat, if rocky, but outside the hillfort, to the north-east, the hill-slope rises, in effect overlooking it from quite close to. However, serious defence was certainly intended, for where the wall is least diminished, on the north side, it is very substantial with some of the upright revetting stones still in place. Entrances were on the north-west and south-east, the latter still with some approach-walling in place. The stone footings of round-houses built against the inside of the rampart are discernible amongst the fallen rubble, but the suspiciously cosy-looking shelters on the outside of the north-west wall are attributed to modern picnickers! The rampart has been extensively robbed on the south-west, and here and on the east side has collapsed downhill.

111. Mynydd Caregog; SN 04163652: The grassy track through the heather from Bedd Morris to Carn Ingli runs right across this large hut circle, c. 60ft in diameter. The circle appears as two distinct ridges in the path about two thirds of the distance from the car park to the point where (a little way to the right) a wire fence encloses the northernmost sector of the forestry plantation.

112. Mynydd Melyn; SN 027362: A settlement site, including a large grass-covered circular enclosure 50ft in diameter and levelled into the hill-slope, a circular hut site 25ft in diameter and a rectangular hut, 15 x 6ft. All are taken to be pre-historic. The area is crossed by the footpath from Bedd Morris stone due westwards to the north side of the summit of Mynydd Melyn. The site is just west of the crossing of this path with the one running north/south. From the gate on the east side of the saddle, follow the wire fence a short distance south to the second gate, and from there strike due east. The enclosures are about 100 yards into the moorland. On the northern slope below the north/south path is a hut circle at c.SN 034370, and two field-systems, one on the north flank of the hill and the other to the west, at SN 023367, but they are not easily accessible.

113. Carn Enoch; SN 01263705: This roundel is now thought to be a ring-cairn, but is also recorded as an Iron Age hut-circle. It is very visible, just below Carn Enoch crags, slightly downhill to the east. See the photograph on p. 78.

114-16 : A line of three defended sites above the Gwaun. It is possible that **116** is the earliest, followed by **115**, and that **114** is not pre-Roman. All three seem to have taken advantage of a remarkably defensible locality as need arose. At the time of writing these sites are inaccessible, and the surrounding footpaths not exactly as shown on the map. Irritatingly, they cannot be seen from any of the roads above or along the Gwaun!

114. Allt Penrhiw; SN 03033408: A rectangular enclosure on a scarp edge defended by double banks up to 2.5m high. Rounded corners suggest that this is a later, Romano-British work.

115. Allt Pengegin Isaf; SN 03133403: A late Iron Age homestead, levelled inside, protected by rock-cut ditches and an impressive upstanding bank. There is a small outwork to the south-west.

116. Castell Pengegin; SN 03903440: A triangular and classic promontory fort on high ground above very steep slopes. Double banks and ditches with a bank-top to ditch-bottom fall of up to 5m defend the 'landward' side. The small footpath running west from just west of the Nature Trail does not go right past the fort as indicated, but from the top of the ascent the lines of the ramparts can be seen on the next bluff to the west. (The original path is still there, but not signposted as usable.)

117. Llanychaer; SM 986353: A defended enclosure with a brief additional outer bank. Just behind the village pub. There is no access but the site is visible from the roadside. There is a splendid view of the surrounding banks from the steep bit of road beyond the bridge on the other side of the river. (See the picture on p. 57.)

118. Tregynon; SN 05253452: A minute defended enclosure with a later mediaeval structure within. It is perched on a precipice surrounded by a deep water-logged ditch 3-4 ft wide and an upstanding rampart up to 10ft high. Entrance at the south end. The defences are tree-covered but visible and very impressive. A delightful spot! There is a full information board including a plan. Access is along the designated footpath leading off Tregynon Country Hotel driveway (signposted), which lies at the extreme end of the unnumbered road half-way between Cilgwyn and Pontfaen.

119. Carn Fuwch; SN 02432912: An enclosure, c. 65 x 80m, with big bold banks. The multiple defences are blurred in places where disturbed by quarrying. The outer banks are visible to the north and south-east, and there are possible traces of an annexe to the south. The dating is uncertain, but is taken as Iron Age. The site is partly visible from the road-bank immediately east of Castlebythe cross-roads, and from the unenclosed land uphill of the enclosure.

120. Bernard's Well Mountain; SN 057294: Hut enclosure and field-systems. This is a large stone-built settlement, with the remains of hut walls on the east side of the site, fields to the west, and walls upstanding to over 18ins high. Although there is a footpath from Dyffryn Syfynwy north across the fields to the B4329, it is not presently marked at either end, and runs below the convex contours so that, exasperatingly, little can actually be seen from it. The only viewing points from ground level are the reservoir gateway on the east side of the B4329 just south of the hill's dome, and the beginning of the private lane (please, no cars) leading up towards Ty Rhig. Neither is very good, but in optimal conditions (drought/frost/slanting sunlight) some of the nearer walls and settlement patterns can be discerned.

121. Caer, Bayvil; SN 11244171: An Iron Age enclosure later used as an Early Christian cemetery in the sixth century AD. A trial excavation in 1979 indicated an early palisaded site with two or three subsequent phases. The banks of the round enclosure are still quite high, with an entrance to the south-west. The site is rather out of the area, but is included as one of the few open lowland defended settlements that can be easily seen. There is an excellent view from the road-bank, but no public access. The enclosure is right beside a small road leading north off the B4582, half way between Nevern and Croft.

IRON AGE SITES:
800 BC - AD56

122. Cwm Gloyne; SN 10403965: A small promontory fort on a steep side valley just downstream from the major site at Castell Henllys. Built in an unusual 'W' shape occupying two natural spurs, it is defended on the 'inland' side by a single bank and ditch. It can be dimly seen in winter through the trees to the right of the top of the signposted footpath from Felindre Farchog, and extending into the pasture, but the path does not come right up to it.

123. Castell Henllys; SN 117391: A large multi-phase hillfort, open to the public from spring to autumn. There is a Visitor Centre and facilities run by the Pembrokeshire Coast National Park. On-going training excavations, which take place every summer, have revealed old ground surfaces, sections, post-holes, walls etc., which can be seen from public walkways and viewing points.

The defensible siting of the fort makes itself felt by the uphill approach to the main gate, which is protected by a nastily effective *chevaux de frise*, not as deep as that at Carn Alw (**133**) but with more jagged upright stones. Imagining trying to ride a horse, or even to run on foot through it, is a better way of demonstrating how it works than any verbal description. Quite a distance behind this (again in contrast to Carn Alw) is a complex entrance, a massive gateway with two pairs of successive semi-circular guard-chambers behind it on either side of a metalled passage. A hoard of slingstones, buried by later works, similarly suggests that at this stage defence was a genuine priority. The ramparts use the natural contours to enhance their height and exaggerate the effect of the ditch depth. This phase of the fort has been given as the 5th century BC.

The defences were re-designed and altered several times. Walling constrained the bank material in places, repaired as and where needed, and wooden palisade fences were built and re-built along the bank-top. At one point the first entrance was fired, but without leaving traces of offensive action, so it may have been no more than purposeful demolition in pre-paration for re-building. This took place after a period of abandonment, and it may be that this second major occupation and reconstruction were less militaristic and more declamatory. The entrance was altered, the *chevaux de frise* covered over with an outer bank, and the guard-chambers re-duced to one, larger pair. The slingstone hoard was abandoned beneath the foundations of a stone work which may have been linked by a wooden superstructure to the gate-tower, and at some point the defences around the whole hilltop were enhanced and

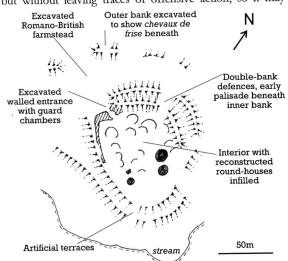

Features of Castell Henllys as known at the end of the 1998 digging season. (After Mytum 1991 and 1998, and site information board.)

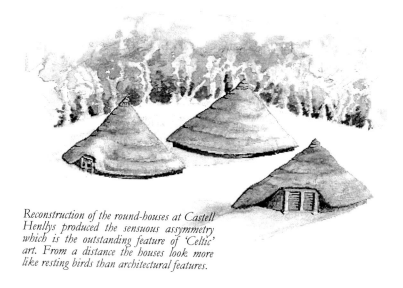

Reconstruction of the round-houses at Castell Henllys produced the sensuous assymmetry which is the outstanding feature of 'Celtic' art. From a distance the houses look more like resting birds than architectural features.

refurbished. A few sherds of pottery (rare in West Wales at this time), some glass beads, the slag from bronze-working and the corroded remains of hunting spears indicate that this was a wealthy, high-status residence. There are surprisingly few four-poster 'store-houses'; these, and parts of a single quern, all date from the later phases of the fort. Carbonised grain increases in quantity in the later periods. This all suggests that at the height of its grandeur Castell Henllys was a tribute-receiving centre, probably given over to élite pursuits rather than base economics. Other finds of spindle-whorls, iron sickle fragments and abundant sheep-bones, which might belie this impression, have not been published as coming from datable contexts.

Further phases of rebuilding followed, with diminishing significance, until the fort was abandoned altogether, perhaps in favour of the enclosed settlements which are so predominant a feature of the Late Iron Age. Finally the defences were used to enclose a small Romano-British settlement, set between the outer bank covering the *chevaux de frise* and the old gateway.

Excavation showed the interior to be crowded with the gullies and postholes of round-houses of various phases. It now contains reconstructions of four of them (one of which is unusually large), all re-built on their original foundations. For anyone who has been pursuing the Iron Age of the bleak hut-circles and ruined walls on the hillsides, these are

A fragment of an 'involuted' brooch was found at Castell Henllys. This complete example is from Oxfordshire. (After Harding in Megaw & Simpson, 1981.)

IRON AGE SITES:
800 BC - AD56

The early pig was a mean, lean pork. Bred from captured wild swine, they kept the mane of bristles along the spine, the straight tail, coarse-haired skin and striped bonhams of their wild cousins. Today's pig is a selectively bred descendent of an Asiatic type, introduced in modern times.

fascinating and, at quiet times, most evocative buildings, very sheltered and curiously spacious with high, elaborate roof-frames and lazily smouldering central hearths. Occasional feasts and festivals are held in and around them, and they are supplemented by reproduced animal pens with Soay sheep and back-bred pigs, smithing furnaces, upright looms, woodwork and other domestic Iron Age equipment, all made on the site. Guidebooks are available, and there are numerous comprehensive information boards. Just north-west of the hillfort another site, Henllys Top Field, is under investigation. The indications are that a late homestead may have been located here (related to the abandonment of the hillfort?).

124-6. Penybenglog forts. None of these has been excavated, and nothing except a few undatable flints has been found in the area. A magnificent view of their 'promontory' aspect can be had from the Crosswell-Newport minor road on the left bank of the Nyfer. The two promontory forts are perched high above precipitous, tree-covered cliffs, and the dome of Castell Mawr is on the skyline behind and between them.

124. Castell Llwyd, SN 11263762: A classically situated small pear-shaped bracken and grass covered promontory fort overlooking the A. Nyfer. There are remains of hut circles in the interior. The eastern foot of the fort is passed by a well-marked footpath leading steeply up from Troed y Rhiw, on the Nevern, to above the site at Penybenglog Farm, east of Felindre Farchog on the A487. There is a really fine view of the ditches and ramparts from the part of the path immediately above the small gate at the top of the steep ascent (less clear in summer foliage). Well worth seeing, to appreciate the fort's promontory position from above. It is a somewhat eerie experience to walk north along Penybenglog track to the main road, straight towards the Iron Age roofs of the round-houses at Henllys - a sight worth enjoying.

125. Castell Mawr, SN 11883778: A small hillfort on the dome of a discreet rise. It has two rings of bank and ditch defences, and the outer ditch is rock-cut with a bank still up to 3m high. The approach was possibly walled, and the interior is divided by a cross-bank. The entrance is to the east.

126. Penybenglog promontory fort, SN 11883728: This is defended by double ditches on the 'inland' side; the outer ditch is cut into the living rock.

127. Tycanol, SN 091367: Impressive promontory site, seriously defended by rock-cut ditches, heavy stone walling and interior dry-stone divisions. The wood is a lichen reserve (over 400 species grow here) in the care of the Countryside Commission for Wales, and visitors are restricted to the marked paths. The Iron Age site cannot be entered, but stands above and to the right of that section of the path from Tycanol Farm to Carnedd Meibion Owen where it rises steeply through the trees. The path passes the approach to the entrance, which can be seen as a rising terrace running north-west uphill. It then 'dog-legs' right-handed around the defences, which can be glimpsed in winter through the trees on the level ground at the top. A visit gives meaning to the name 'promontory' fort, and a vivid impression of the difference in the landscape between today's artificial 'reserves' and the Iron Age defended subsistence core-land. (See the photograph on page 58.)

128-9. Banc Llwydlos; SN 09303311 and **Foel Eryr; SN 069319**: Two sites of possible hut circles and open settlements. Both are hard to spot on the hillsides, especially the former. Their prehistoric status has been questioned.

Stretch of Iron Age settlement walling at Waun Clyn Coch.

130. Waun Clyn Coch; SN 10673134: A large and well preserved enclosed settlement of Iron Age/Romano-British date. Most of the boundary wall is traceable, and the entrances are to the north-west and south-east. There are ten to twelve hut-circles inside, and more outside to the north. The site is in rough pasture, rather smothered in summer. It is quite a long walk along the track opposite Glynsaithmaen farm, from where permission and directions must be sought. There is an excellent bird's eye view of the settlement from the southern slopes of Foel Feddau, especially in frost. It is remarkably well worth seeing.

131. Croesmihangel; SN 168333: An undated enclosure revealed by aerial photography. If it were verified as Iron Age, it would be interestingly close to Foel Drygarn.

132. Foel Drygarn; SN 15773360: Because of its spectacular position at the end of the Preseli range, Foel Drygarn is the best known and most visited site in the area. The three formidable cairns from which it takes its name stand proud above the ramparts, and are a landmark for miles around. These Bronze Age cairns occupy so much space in the middle of the hillfort that questions about their credentials have been raised - however, they are so like the other Bronze Age cairns on the hill-tops (see p. 38) that it seems more likely that they are just that and not collapsing Iron

**IRON AGE SITES:
800 BC - AD56**

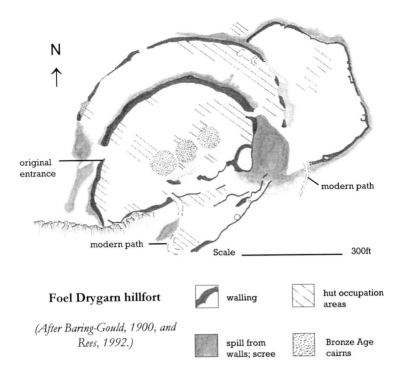

original entrance

modern path

modern path

Scale ———————————— 300ft

Foel Drygarn hillfort

(After Baring-Gould, 1900, and Rees, 1992.)

walling

hut occupation areas

spill from walls; scree

Bronze Age cairns

Age look-outs or signal points. Some of the hut-circles seem to pre-date the ramparts; the hillfort is thought to have originated in the Late Bronze Age and to have continued to function, if intermittently, until well into Roman times. Three separate enclosures may represent three stages of expansion outwards from the summit. This first enclosure, containing the cairns, is surrounded by walls joining rocky prominences on the south, and everywhere else by an impressive ditch and bank. The northern stretches of this bank still stand to 3.5m high, and the packed earth and rubble of which they are made can be seen in the scrapes the sheep have hollowed out for shelter. The second enclosure, built in a crescent outside the first, is thought to have been a response to an increase in the overall population in the Iron Age, and has less substantial defences. The succeeding annexe, lower and to the north-west, furthered the process and has quite flimsy walls. It used to be thought that both the later enclosures functioned as stock-pens; presumably in times of danger the people would take refuge on the summit while the sheep, goats and cattle took their chance with the slings and arrows outside them (not consistent with the attitude displayed at Carn Alw!). Aerial photography has revealed numerous hut circles in all three enclosures, although in the outer ones the huts are grouped with plenty of free space for penning.

There can be no doubt that Foel Drygarn was an important centre in Celtic times, with prestige gifts or exchanges speaking of far-flung contacts. Early exploration of the hillfort produced a few but quite significant finds (see pp. 61-2). These include scraps of what is probably a style of pottery known as Llanmelin ware, which was

Right: *Excavator extraordinary: Digging out little semi-circular shelters, sheep have revealed urns and flints, soil and rampart sections. Here, at Foel Drygarn, they have preserved the remains of the rampart facing by using the stone courses as dry walk-ways.*

Left: *Fragments of standardised Iron Age 'Llanmelin' wares like these were found on Foel Drygarn. These examples come from Walesland Rath, north-west of Haverfordwest (left), Llanmelin hillfort, Monmouthshire (right), and Coygan Camp, near Laugharne (centre).*

(After G.J. Wainwright, 1971; Nash-Williams, 1933; G.J. Wainwright, 1967.)

in use in the second and early first centuries BC, and would provide proof of occupation when Celtic culture was at its most virile.

133. Carn Alw; SN 13903370: An unusually vigorously protected small enclosure under the lee of the dolerite crag which the defensive wall encloses. A wide *chevaux de frise*, incorporating set and naturally grounded stones in roughly three bands, the loosest in the middle, would have prohibited any formal attack on the south-east, where the approach is level and easy. (See the photograph on p. 59.) On all other sides the defensive wall enhances the natural rock formation and so did not need to be as elaborately protected. The only other *chevaux de frise* in Preseli is at Castell Henllys (**123**), where it forms part of the early defence-work, obliterated by a later bank. If, as has been suggested, they both belong to a temporal 'trend' in defence works, then Carn Alw should be early, too. However, the device was widespread in time and space in western Europe, and it need not be assumed that the two Preseli examples are contemporary. (The Romans developed the stone form into batches of hideously sharpened stakes set in the bottoms of ditches). The single and apparently simple entrance is approached through the *chevaux de frise* by a heavy boulder-lined lane-way which has been blocked half way along and re-directed in a curve, thus making the

**IRON AGE SITES:
800 BC - AD56**

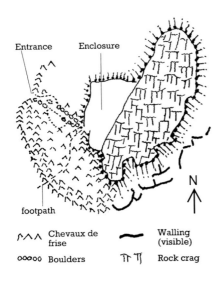

Entrance   Enclosure

footpath

| ∧∧∧ | Chevaux de frise | ▬ | Walling (visible) |
| ooooo | Boulders | 𝍫 𝍫 | Rock crag |

N ↑

Carn Alw

(After Mytum & Webster, 1989)

approach even more devious. Despite these elaborate precautions, there is absolutely no sign of structures or even occupation within. The defended area is a small, triangular, paddock-like plateau, covering a mere 30 x 50 metres, which has led to the suggestion that it may be a stockpen. If so there must have been something peculiarly valuable about the stock kept there. A spindle whorl found near Carn Alw, and said to have been decorated with concentric circles (a frequently-used Iron Age design) joined by 'cross-lines', inevitably evokes a picture of Celtic women spinning wool plucked from sheep in the fortress-fold; but if Carn Alw is a stock-enclosure, bulls or horses would seem more likely incumbents.

Around the south and south-east of the crag there are extensive field-systems which may have originated in the late Bronze Age, with a possible unenclosed Late Bronze Age type of settlement as their focus. Another enclosure to the north may have succeeded the main 'hillfort'.

Carn Alw. The main entry through the chevaux de frise is lined with heavy boulders, creating an unusually formidable approach.

134. Craig Talfynedd; SN 133313: A significant complex of shelters, hut standings, walls and terraces. These are almost impossible to decipher at ground level among naturally scattered boulders. The site is best approached along the mountain track around the south-east foot of Carn Sian.

135. Castell Garw; SN 14722690: This was previously recorded as a possible henge (see p. 28), but recent trial excavations have revealed a Late Bronze Age/Early Iron Age defensive site. It is easily seen by mounting the east road-bank of the second field north of Glandy Cross garage - but with caution and tact: the road is very busy in summer, and banks are vulnerable. The site shows up as a large green ring near the left-hand corner of the field. There are records of standing and fallen stones in and beside it, and the relationship of all these seems complex.

Photograph: Ailinor Evans

Preseli ponies, seen here in winter beneath Foel Cwmcerwyn corrie, once the source of an Ice Age glacier. It was ponies like these that drew the chariots and carried the heroes of Celtic battle-lore, and many of them still breed true to the primitive markings and the colours sung in the battle poems.

IRON AGE SITES:
800 BC - AD56

BOOK LIST

There is no general account of the prehistory of Preseli. Most of the professional papers and reports consulted in relation to this little guide book have been published in the three main Welsh archaeological journals: *Archaeologia Cambrensis, Bulletin of the Board of Celtic Studies, Archaeology in Wales.* A full list would be inappropriate here; however, the bibliographies included in the following titles, which may be of interest, will supply most of the references.

Local

George Children & George Nash: *Neolithic Sites of Cardiganshire, Carmarthenshire and Pembrokeshire;* Logaston Press, 1997. Includes useful plans and site lists of megalithic monuments.

John, Brian: *Walking in the Presely Hills;* Pembrokeshire Coast National Park Authority, revised ed. 1993. Includes much interesting geological information on the hill walks.

Rees, Sian: *A Guide to Ancient and Historic Wales - Dyfed;* Cadw 1992. The official field-guide to the major monuments in West Wales in the care of Cadw (Scheduled Monuments only). Bibliography of excavation reports etc. of sites included.

*

Kirk, T. & Williams, G.: 'Glandy Cross: a later prehistoric monumental complex in Carmarthenshire, Wales'; in *Proceedings of the Prehistoric Society*, 2000, vol. 66. A detailed professional paper on the latest results and analyses from Glandy Cross.

Lynch, F.M.: 'Portal Dolmens in the Nevern Valley'; in ed. Lynch, F.M. & Burgess, C.B.: *Prehistoric Man in Wales and the West;* Adams & Dart, 1972. Professional essay on the chronology and relationships of the dolmens, on which most later interpretations are based.

Wales

Lynch, Frances, Aldhouse-Green, Stephen and Davies, Jeffrey L.: *Prehistoric Wales,* Sutton 2000. A complete and up to date account of Welsh prehistory. Accessible text, fully illustrated with photographs, plans, drawings, maps and tables. Extensive bibliography.

General:

Darvill, Timothy: *Prehistoric Britain;* Routledge, 1987. Provides an excellent general background to the specifically Welsh books above; unusually informative on Welsh material. Comprehensively illustrated; themed select bibliography.

Evans, John G.: *Land and Archaeology*, Tempus 1999. Series of close-up environmental studies of localities for those interested in the ecological history of special places.

The Sites and Monuments Record of the Dyfed Archaeological Trust (Pembrokeshire, Carmarthenshire and Ceredigion) is held by Cambria Archaeology, in Llandeilo; the National Monuments Record is held by the Royal Commission on Ancient and Historical Monuments in Wales, in Aberystwyth. Both Records are available for genuine consultation.

ACKNOWLEDGEMENTS

We are most grateful to:

Eleanor Breen, of the Sites and Monuments Record of the Dyfed Archaeological Trust, and the staff of the National Monuments Record (Royal Commission on the Ancient and Historical Monuments of Wales) for giving unstintingly of their time and knowledge in the assembly of the site list.

Trevor Kirk for pre-publication information on the contents and implications of his recent paper on Glandy Cross.

Ailinor Evans for days spent in bittter cold weather, when the gorse and bracken were low, photographing sites for us.

David Jacobs and Steve Twohill (COLOUR DIVISION, 168, West End Lane, London NW6 1SD) for invaluable help and advice.

We are wholly indebted to the numerous scholars and researchers, and excavators and draughtsmen who have worked in Preseli. Their numerous individual contributions on the sites and finds of the area rise literally into the hundreds, and it would be invidious to select some at the expense of others.

Finally, but primarily, we would like to express our gratitude to the many landholders who have given us permission to visit sites on private land, and who have so often taken time to accompany us around their farms in enthusiastic participation in this venture.

INDEX

*

Other titles from Atelier Productions:

Dead Men's Boats: The Early Mediaeval Canoe from Llangorse, and the sunken dugouts of Wales and the Marches.
ISBN 1 899793 02 X

The Romans in Breconshire and Radnorshire: a field guide.
ISBN 1 899793 00 3

Welsh Prehistory: Catalogue of accessions in the county and local museums of Wales, and other collections.
ISBN 1 899793 05 4

Y Gaer: Brecon Roman Fort
ISBN 1 899793 01 1

ATELIER PRODUCTIONS
2, Bontfaen, Forge,
Machynlleth, Powys SY20 8RN

atelier_productions@yahoo.co.uk

Front cover: Cerrig Meibion Arthur (see p. 96)
Back cover: Carn Ingli from the east (see p. 101)